Date Due

COLUMBIA UNIVERSITY SLAVONIC STUDIES

DEMOCRATIC IDEAS IN TURGENEV'S WORKS

DEMOCRATIC IDEAS IN TURGENEV'S WORKS

BY

HARRY HERSHKOWITZ

INSTRUCTOR IN THE MODERN LANGUAGE DEPARTMENT OF
JAMES MONROE HIGH SCHOOL, NEW YORK

NEW YORK
COLUMBIA UNIVERSITY PRESS
1932

Copyright 1932
COLUMBIA UNIVERSITY PRESS

Published August, 1932

PRINTED IN THE UNITED STATES OF AMERICA
GEORGE BANTA PUBLISHING COMPANY, MENASHA, WISCONSIN

TO MY WIFE

PREFACE

Much interest has been aroused in Russian books among the English speaking public since the appearance of such excellent translations of the works of Tolstoy, Dostoyevsky, and Turgenev as those of Constance Garnett and Isabel F. Hapgood. Other translators have been encouraged to widen the scope and thus to bring home to English readers the richness of a literature that is second to none. And yet there are many groundless prejudices entertained with respect to the character of the Russian people. It is hoped that this book will help to dispel some of these prejudices and will contribute toward a more sympathetic knowledge of this nation.

Turgenev is one of the three greatest Russian prose writers; as a stylist, he is perhaps the greatest. The aesthetic quality of his writings has long been recognized. On the other hand, few have pointed out Turgenev's place as a fighter for liberty, a characteristic so strongly in evidence in his works.

During the course of my researches my wife, who became an enthusiastic admirer of Turgenev, has been a constant source of inspiration. Her views, coming from one who was born and reared on American soil, frequently suggested to me new angles of vision.

I wish to express my acknowledgments to Professor Manning of Columbia University, with whom I spent many delightful hours in discussions while the work was in preparation.

My thanks are also due to Dr. Coleman of Columbia University and to Professor Manckiewicz of the College of the City of New York, for occasional criticisms.

Lastly, I feel that I owe a debt of gratitude to Miss Wallace of the Columbia University Press for her painstaking reading of the manuscript and for her preparation of it for the press.

H. Hershkowitz

New York City
    April, 1932

CONTENTS

CHAPTER I

EVOLUTION OF RUSSIAN SERFDOM AND
ITS FINAL ABOLITION

Although the legal conversion of the theoretically free Russian peasant did not become a fact till the second quarter of the seventeenth century,[1] its germs can be traced to conditions in mid-sixteenth century Russia. In 1552 Ivan IV succeeded in pushing the Tatars back toward the southeast, thus clearing the eastern Russian border. New fertile lands attracted floods of immigrants, most of whom arrived without means. Compelled to borrow, they pledged themselves to pay their debts with the returns from the lands upon which they settled. The paying back proved to be a difficult matter and the peasant became fastened to the land, virtually a slave.[2]

When the burdens grew too heavy, there was only one thing left to do: to flee and assume obligations with a new landowner. After a few decades the number who fled and changed landowners became so great that the attention of the central authorities had to be called to the seriousness of the situation. Boris Godunov therefore issued a decree in 1597 intended as a temporary measure of relief whereby peasants who had fled after September 1592 could be reclaimed.[3] The legalization took place between 1620-1650, during the reign of Michael Romanov.[4]

When Peter the Great ascended the throne, he found Russia almost ruined by past wars. One may get an idea of the ferocity of these struggles by reading Sienkiewicz' account in *With Fire and Sword* or, from the Russian side, Gogol's *Taras Bulba*. As a rule

[1] Klyuchevsky, *Kurs russkoi istorii* (A course in Russian History; Lecture XXXVII).

[2] Beazley, Forbes, and Birkett, *Russia from the Varangians to the Bolsheviks*, pp. 115-16, 141.

[3] *Ibid.*, p. 138.   [4] *Ibid.*, p. 141.

buildings were set afire, property was plundered or totally destroyed, cattle were carried away or slaughtered. Not infrequently part of the population was driven out and sold in slave markets.[5] During the fifteenth, sixteenth, and seventeenth centuries such raids were made periodically by the Tatars.[6] To give protection to the frontiers, the government had to build outposts extending for hundreds of miles. A large army of men was needed for the yearly mobilization of the various frontiers. More and more military colonies were consequently found necessary to serve as a protective fence. The only capital that the government could use for the upkeep of the large army consisted of enormous stretches of land, partly peopled by peasants, partly waste. It was this capital that the government had to exploit for purposes of maintaining the large military "serving" class, turning over to them a large part of the tillable soil as military benefices or as hereditary estates.[7] In the interests of national defense as well as to prevent tax losses from change of domicile the peasants were gradually bound to the land and given over to their masters into personal bondage.

During Catherine's reign no measures were taken to alleviate the conditions of the bonded peasant. It was during this period that the growing culture of the nobleman brought with it wants that were out of keeping with former primitive modes of existence. The satisfaction of these wants called for larger outlays of money, which led to a more intense exploitation of the peasant. His legal status grew considerably worse, whereas the bondage right of the noble widened in scope. Although the abnormality of the bondage system was admitted in principle, it was then that the idea of self-liberation began to arouse the minds of the thinking class and to circulate publicly.

The enormity of the abuse becomes apparent when one studies the census toward the end of the eighteenth century. The figures show that of the 12,126,498 comprising the total rural male population no less than 6,678,239, or about 55 per cent, were landowners' bond-

[5] *Ibid.*, p. 110.   [6] *Ibid.*, p. 112.
[7] *Ibid.*, pp. 114-15.
Kornilov, *Kurs istorii Rossii XIX vieka*, I, 26.
Mavor, *An Economic History of Russia*, I, 592.

age peasants.[8] Legally the serf had no rights whatsoever. The landowners assumed the right to control freely the labor of their bonded peasants, whom they could transfer from the soil to house service, could sell singly or with their families, or could lend to others. Their power to punish them was abused shamefully. Not infrequently did the owners put them into domestic prisons and inflict severe corporal punishment upon them for relatively trifling transgressions, or merely for insolent behavior.

This extension of the nobleman-landowner's rights over the peasant was not always accompanied by an extension of his own obligations toward the government. Whereas in Peter's day a nobleman had to attain a rank in service, as a condition of holding his social status, this tradition continued only in name in Catherine's reign, since nobles were freed from obligations in peace times by her husband, Peter III.

Under Catherine the landowners were allowed to exile their serfs to hard-labor prisons. Long before that time the masters had appropriated the right to interfere in family life, to marry by force, to dispose of property.[9] Again and again in Turgenev's works we shall have occasion to refer to abuses that were almost unbelievable. At the same time the serfs were forbidden to complain against their masters. That the serfs did not resignedly accept such conditions is evidenced by complaints sent to the Government, by uprisings, by assassinations of landowners. Sometimes the unrest would embrace considerable territories, and could only be quelled by military repressions, executions, whippings, and exile. At Catherine's accession some 150,000 peasants took part in uprisings. Besides government officials, 1,572 landlords were reported killed.[10] In 1773 the Pugachev insurrection grew to enormous dimensions, seriously threatening the existence of the state.[11]

When we reach the nineteenth century we find that the abolition of serfdom becomes the chief event of internal Russian history. His-

[8] Henri Storch, *Cours d'economie politique, ou exposition des principes qui déterminent la prospérité des nations*, VI, 272 (Figures for the year 1782).

[9] Serfdom was legalized during the reign of Tsar Michael Romanov (1613-45), (see page 1).

[10] Massaryk, *The Spirit of Russia*, p. 71.

[11] Beazley, Forbes, and Birkett, *op. cit.*, p. 319.

torians consider this event of such great moment that as a rule they divide Russian history in the nineteenth century into two periods, one leading up to the Abolition of Serfdom and one treating of the subsequent period. This event is considered as a starting point for the work of liberating the entire population.

When Alexander I ascended the throne he gave evidence of liberal inclinations by a few imperial acts, such as his manifesto liberating a number of political prisoners[12] and his constitutions to Poland[13] and to Finland[14]. He was a weak-willed sentimentalist, however, who could easily be brought under the influence of reactionary leaders of the worst type, notably Arakcheyev,[15] an extreme militarist, who, it seems, held the Emperor's confidence by dint of his flattery and by a pietistic attitude.

The first attempt at the liberation of the peasants took place in the early reign of Alexander I by an imperial edict of February 20, 1803, concerning Free Agriculture.[16] The law allowed serf-owners to liberate their bondmen individually, or by whole villages, not otherwise than with land allotments under conditions arrived at by mutual agreement between the owners and their serfs. The peasants thus liberated were called Free Agriculturists, and the Government could not dispose of their land. A year later, the next peasant measure was issued[17] concerning itself with the peasants of the province of Lifland. According to this regulation, it was forbidden to sell or pledge peasants without land; the peasants received personal rights and a certain amount of self-government; they became the hereditary owners of their land portions, which they could lose only by the verdict of the court; finally, the peasants could be punished only by verdict of the district court. A year later a similar measure was promulgated for the province of Estland.

In general, we may say that Alexander I adopted a liberal attitude toward the peasant question. He gave attention to peasants' complaints against their landowners and inflicted severe punishments upon guilty owners, depriving them frequently of the management

---

[12] *Ibid.*, p. 354.   [13] *Ibid.*, p. 388.

[14] *Ibid.*, p. 388.   [15] *Ibid.*, pp. 381, 385.

[16] Kovalevsky, *Modern Customs and Ancient Laws of Russia*, p. 221.

[17] Ukase of Feb. 20, 1804. Kornilov, *op. cit.*, I, 126.

of their estates.[18] No radical changes, however, were made during his reign and peasant-uprisings continued in the reign of Nicholas I. The government had to keep strict vigilance, until about the middle of the nineteenth century, when new circumstances of great import accelerated the solution of the problem. New material conditions sprang up in the national life and these prepared the way for the downfall of serfdom more promptly than any uprisings or idealistic demands could have done.

First and foremost of the causes that led up to it was the increased density of the population which rendered bondage labor very unprofitable for the landowners, since there was a surplus of hands for the primitive farming that was resorted to in those days. Very little was known about scientific methods of farming whereby the product per average unit of soil could be increased. Forced labor did not allow any real intensification of the production of the soil. The growth of the bonded population increased considerably within the two decades between 1815 and 1835—by more than a million souls.[19] The excessive number of serfs became a problem to landowners. The only thing they could do was to transfer the peasants into the class of house-serfs whose support had to be provided for and whose productivity was nothing. By 1835 we find that out of the ten million bondsmen more than one million were house-serfs. This number kept on increasing.

These serfs were treated by the landowners without ceremony. Many were driven out to beg. The more enterprising landowners tried to employ their surplus hands in estate-factories which had begun to spring up by the end of the eighteenth century. These factories, however, met later a strong competition on the part of the merchant factories whose technical improvements were of a higher order. Before long, possessors of estate factories came to the conclusion that forced labor was not profitable, because of the inefficiency of the factory hands and of the administration.

Besides the increase in the density of the population referred to

[18] A characteristic allusion to such interference on the part of the Crown, even in Catherine's reign, is seen in Fonvizin's *Nyedorosl* ("The Minor"); in *Pervoye polnoye sobraniye sochinenii D. I. Fonvizina*, p. 156.

[19] Mavor, *op. cit.*, I. 418.

above, landowners suffered from heavy indebtedness, as a result of the Napoleonic wars. More than half of the estates were mortgaged to credit institutions at high rates of interest.[20] These combined conditions caused financial deficits that were ever increasing. The relation between peasants and their masters became aggravated thereby. During the forties, Ryazan and Orel began to feel that the liquidation of serfdom would be more profitable.

In so far as the peasants are concerned, they, too, felt that the situation had become intolerable. During the reign of Nicholas I there were no less than five hundred and fifty-six peasant disturbances, frequently involving districts of several villages. The last seven years of his reign saw one hundred and thirty-seven disturbances.[21] About half of these uprisings had to be quelled by military force, with frequent bloodshed.

The attitude of the Russian intelligentsia toward the question deserves attention. During the forties there began to appear in the capitals and provinces circles of progressive young men, among whom not only all sorts of social and literary problems were discussed, but also the political issues of the day. The serf question came in for its due share of attention in these discussions. Almost all the circles knew one another and kept up mutual relations. Each member became a center of propaganda, the views of the day thus spreading in geometric ratio. It is only natural to expect that the liberation of the serfs should find in the intelligentsia strong advocates, inasmuch as the majority of students belonged to one circle or another. The censorship found it necessary to increase its vigilance over the press and the writings of the literary figures of the day. Turgenev was arrested in 1852 and kept at a police-station for an attempt to evade the watchfulness of the censor.

Early in his reign, in 1855-1856 Alexander II achieved the reputation of being a sincere friend of liberal organizations. This fact gave courage to liberal writers of the day. Hertsen, made bold, addressed a letter to the monarch in which he spoke of the needs of Russia: the liberation of the peasants by the landowners, the liberation of the tax-paying classes from corporal punishment, and the liberation

[20] *Ibid.*, I, 520-23.   [21] Kornilov, *op. cit.*, II, 46.

of the press from censorship. In his peace-manifesto, Alexander II spoke of the equalization of classes, which many interpreted as a hint at the liberation of the serfs.[22] In his speech to the nobles he said that he found that the existing conditions must not continue and that it would be better to abolish serfdom "from above" than to wait till it abolished itself from below. In spite of all that, the censorship was careful in withholding from the press permission to discuss the bondage problem openly. Yet unofficial leaflets circulated freely and finally forced themselves upon the attention of the Ministry.

In March, 1859, an Editing Commission was established with instructions to draw up statutes dealing with peasant reforms.[23] The commission could not come to a definite agreement and the work advanced slowly. Finally Alexander announced that he would not tolerate any further delay. On January 28, 1861, the Tsar opened the session of the State Council. He delivered a long and vigorous speech in which the peasant-question was reviewed, beginning with preceding reigns. He concluded by giving the State Council time till February 15th, to draw up the document in its final form. On February 19th, the Tsar signed the Act which freed the peasants from personal and legal subjection to the landowners. The chief significance of the abolition of bondage resulted not only in great economic consequences for the peasantry, gentry, and industry of the country, but it paved the way for other reforms.

If we now leave the field of history and look for indications of revolutionary ideas in Russian literature we find that some can be traced back to the eighteenth century. It was a period during which the actions of the aristocracy were characterized by a total absence of any sense of right or wrong. Strongly suggestive of this situation is Kapnist's (1756-1823) *Yabeda* ("Pettifoggery"), a comedy satirizing particularly the abuses of Russian justice.[24] Knyazhnin's (1742-1791) tragedy *Vadim* in which he tries to portray, in dramatic form, the struggle between republican Novgorod and the monarchic Ruric breathes a revolutionary spirit in no veiled terms. Only some time

---

[22] *Ibid.*, II, 134.   [23] *Ibid.*, II, 137.
[24] Wiener, *Anthology of Russian Literature*, I, 309.

after the play was published (1793) did the tendency of its revolutionary utterances become apparent, and the book was ordered to be burnt by the executioner. It was fortunate for the author that he was dead, or he would hardly have escaped severe punishment.

In language equally impressive Radishchev advocated the liberation of the serfs in his *Journey from St. Petersburg to Moscow*, written in 1790.[25] When exiled to Siberia, he continued his literary pursuits, writing an "Ode to Liberty," which is a forerunner of poems on liberty by Ryleyev[26] and Ogarev.[27] Krylov in "Pokhvalnaya ryech' v pamyat' moemu dyedushke" ("A Panegyric of my Grandfather"),[28] considered his best satire, gives a caricature of a rude, selfish and savage country squire who cared more for his hounds and horses than for any of his two thousand serfs. We are told how "noble" an example he would offer by showing how it was possible to apply the rod to each of them two or three times a week, by way of edification.[29]

The horrors of the peasant serf-laws (Krepostnoye pravo) were so appalling that they called forth a reaction among the better type of minds. This reaction found expression in the masonic movement, which was spreading rapidly.

The masons found in Novikov (1744-1818), the first Russian philosopher, a powerful advocate of their ideas.

Novikov began his literary activity early and expressed his views in satiric periodicals[30] that made their appearance early in the reign of Catherine II. He was determined to go beyond light satire: he sought to get at the roots of evil. It was his purpose to point out the demoralizing influences of the then existing slavery upon the higher spheres of society. His periodicals were before long ordered discontinued by the Empress though it was she who originally had a hand in their establishment. She apparently grew alarmed at the possible

[25] *Ibid.*, I, 362-70.

[26] "Voynarovsky," cf. Wiener, *op. cit.*, II, 87-88.

[27] "To Iskander," see *Free Russia*, Vol. XI, No. 11; also Wiener, *op. cit.*, II, 242-43.

[28] Wiener, *op. cit.*, I, 283.

[29] Krylov, *Polnoye sobraniye sochinenii*, III, 284.

[30] *Truten* ("The Drone") 1769-70; *Zhivopisets* ("The Painter") 1772-73; *Moskovskiya Vyedomosti* ("Moscow Gazette") 1779-89.

consequences. Nevertheless, during the short while that his pen was active, he was able through these periodicals to influence a large portion of the thinking population.

Shortly after the discontinuance of the periodicals, Novikov opened a large printing and publishing house, with a view to publishing and spreading books of a philosophic and moral nature. Being an extremely active person and not devoid of business acumen, he was able to interest booksellers throughout Russia. His influence upon the educated spheres came to be considerable. As it was not the sort of influence that the Empress favored, a means was sought to make him harmless. A pretext to arrest him was soon found on grounds of his having been mixed up in a political conspiracy. He was confined in the Schlisselberg Fortress in 1792, to remain there for fifteen years. Four years later, however, upon the accession of Paul I, he was set free. Catherine's attitude toward Novikov is somewhat surprising in view of the fact that she gave plentiful evidence of liberal inclinations. She was familiar with Locke and other revolutionary thinkers and prided herself on possessing a liberty-loving character. At one time she even seriously contemplated peasant reforms, but these did not go beyond founding in 1765 the "Free Economic Society" one of the functions of which was to study the question of liberating the peasants.

About 1780 Count Panin, envoy to Sweden, had D. I. Fonvizin, his secretary, draw up a plan based largely upon Rousseau's *Social Contract* and foreshadowing the liberation of the peasants. Although it had the approval of Paul and of certain leading members of the nobility it led to no practical results. Moreover, in a charter granted to the aristocracy in 1785[31] in which the right to hold assemblies was accorded to them, the welfare of the peasant was completely overlooked. He was made subject to his owner exclusively.

It was about this time that Karamzin was writing his "Poor Liza." In this work he describes the sufferings of a poor peasant girl, who fell in love with a nobleman, and who, being abandoned by him, drowned herself. To be sure, the novel was nothing but one of the many examples of the sentimental romanticism that were then the

[31] Massaryk, *op. cit.*, p. 70.

vogue in western Europe. But inasmuch as the sufferer was the poor peasant girl and the cause of her suffering was a nobleman, it had a tendency to attract sympathy for the poor peasant folk. Some critics[32] consider that its very suggestiveness was, among other factors, a link in the protest against serf-laws, a protest we shall later find so strongly voiced in Turgenev's works.

The Napoleonic Wars that involved Russia during that period could not pass without leaving their influence upon the nation. During the occupation of Paris, Russian soldiers became acquainted with the ideas of freedom current among the Frenchmen. By this time Novikov's liberal ideas commenced to gain ground in Russia. Among other factors one cannot overlook, in this connection, the establishment of numerous secret societies, for the purpose of spreading notions which had for their primary object the abolishing of inequality before the law and the doing away with absolutism.

[32] Kropotkin, *Ideals and Realities in Russian Literature*, p. 33.

Chapter II

EARLY INFLUENCES: 1818-1850

The *milieu* into which Turgenev was born led him to discover his mission, although for a long while he had to grope till he could find himself. His works are decidedly a product of his environment, each one of his major writings being a close representative of the spirit of the times and of the leading ideas that stirred men's minds during the period, especially the minds of the intellectual class in Russia who found spokesmen among such figures as Hertsen, Bakunin, and Byelinsky. His blood-ties threw him into surroundings where the landed proprietor was the lord and where the peasants upon the soil were little more than chattel slaves. Turgenev felt smothered in this environment and longed to break away from it into a freer life upon the continent. Western progress and Western civilization held out many temptations to him. He vowed to fight against the enemy—serfdom. Too weak to grapple with the monster he sought spiritual support in the companionship of other intellectuals of like mind. He met later the great critic Byelinsky who acted in no small measure as a spur upon his activity.

No sooner did Turgenev enter the battlefield, than he had to face the censorship—a staunch supporter of the Serf Law. Upon every corner this many-headed hydra stood sentinel, and yet Turgenev succeeded now and then in escaping the censor's taboo. He gave his enemy a death blow with his *Sportsman's Diary,* stories like "The Inn," "The Office," and "Mumu," and portrayed the period of serfdom with a mastery that has never been surpassed. During the sixty-five years of his life (1818-1883) Turgenev witnessed the Revolutions of 1830, 1848, 1871. A sensitive nature like his could not pass through life without feeling the influence of these events.

The estate upon which Turgenev was born had laid its imprint upon him for the rest of his life. We find him reproducing the scenery, the people, hunting excursions, and association with the peasant-serfs many years after leaving his native home. Some of his stories go back to family traditions. These formed a fund that he drew upon in later life. "The Peasant Proprietor Ovsyanikov" . and "Three Portraits" are very suggestive of such traditions. Often, as a child, he was compelled to look for a place of refuge where he might be at a safe distance from his mother's anger. He tried to escape the rod, something that was considered the standard method of the day in rearing children, a method that his mother resorted to continually. He would run frequently to the green orchard to the serf Lobanov, who was not without education of a sort. It was he who taught the young boy Kheraskov's *Rossiada*. The famous and already aging writer of a later day reproduced this Lobanov in his *Punin and Baburin*.[1]

His early recollections of the Lutovinov estate were associated with gloomy pictures of despotism and cruelty. As he witnessed about him a craving for absolute sway over the bonded peasants, who were made to suffer corporal punishment, who were sent to Siberia, and who were deprived of freedom, his mind became filled with those melancholy pictures which he could never forget. This love of absolute control was carried into one's family, to one's children, who were frequently treated in a manner analogous to that used with the serf.[2]

Turgenev's mother was about thirty when she married Sergei Nikolayevich Turgenev, a most handsome officer of twenty-four. He was attracted by her fortune and intended to keep up some of his amorous adventures after marriage. All the time the iron-willed lady fought for supremacy of power over her handsome husband. The picture of his mother, so much in love with power that the least contradiction of her commands may have meant a life of misery for the culprit, was present in Turgenev's mind for many years. Her portrait can be traced in "Mumu," *Punin and Baburin*, and partly in "The Inn," and "The Master's Main Office." She never

[1] Turgenev, *Polnoye sobraniye sochinenii*, Ed. Glazunov, VIII, 52.
[2] This imperious attitude of parents towards children is shown powerfully in Ostrovsky's *Groza* ("The Storm").

grew tired of tormenting her slaves. "Mumu" is supposed to have had an actual occurrence for its basis. Among the serfs there had indeed been a deaf-mute janitor Andrey, known in the story as Gerasim, whose attachment to a dog attracted the little Turgenev's attention. It is his remarkable power of giving objective reality to his subsequent recollections that enabled Turgenev to reproduce early scenes with such vividness.

Turgenev's mother meted out to her serfs with a vengeance all the sufferings of her unhappy married life. She sent two young fellows to Siberia because they forgot to bow to her. "At this very window," Turgenev told in later life, "my mother was sitting. It was summer and the window was open and I was witnessing the unfortunate young fellows who were doomed to Siberia coming over bareheaded, in order to make their final bow and to take leave of her."[3]

When it came to bringing up her son, very few concessions were made. The same cruelty was exercised in unmitigated fashion. "I was flogged almost every day for the merest trifles" says Turgenev.[4] There were a host of gossiping old cronies watching the little fellow and ready to report any "misdeeds" on his part. To the world of fancy the boy looked early for refuge from the gloomy world of slavery. But the sensitive boy closely observed the faces of both slaves and masters and in his heart there grew up an inveterate hatred of serfdom. It became his mental enemy, and his mother by her cruel personal example unconsciously contributed to this growth of hatred for the Lutovinov estate.

Turgenev was sixteen when his father died in 1834. Referring to that time years later he says: "Hatred against the Serf Law was already deeply rooted in me. It was this hatred, among other things, that was responsible for the fact that not even once did I strike anybody, although personally I was brought up by continual blows."[5] This hatred of serfdom was only accentuated by his later stay at the Moscow University and at the University of St. Petersburg.

[3] Quoted from L'vov Rogachevsky, *I. S. Turgenev, Zhizn' i Tvorchestvo*, pp. 27-28.
[4] *Ibid.*, pp. 27-28.   [5] *Ibid.*, p. 29.

There he was brought face to face with the discipline characteristic of the reign of Tsar Nicholas I, when despotism reached its climax. Social life was being smothered by systematic schemes of repression.

In the thirties the Moscow University was, in a large measure, the center of growing youth. Between 1826 and 1834 Lermontov, Aksakov, and Goncharov spent their student days there. The views of the German idealist Schelling seized upon the minds of brilliant youths like Byelinsky and Stankevich. Along with Schelling were being studied Kant, Fichte, and later, Hegel. Byron was a great favorite in Russia, through which the wave of storm and stress had been passing. Pushkin and Lermontov caught much of the spirit. Schiller's *Robbers* was very popular. Zhukovsky's translations contributed to the atmosphere of romanticism, which worked upon the imaginative young Turgenev.

Before these romantic youths of the thirties rose the monster of Despotism with its inhuman serf laws. Their energies were chained. No free action was possible. Hence they turned within and began to strive for self-perfection. That was the time when various student circles sprang up, one of the most prominent of which grouped about the brilliant Stankevich, poet and thinker. Among the members of the circle were Byelinsky, Aksakov, Bakunin, and his talented sisters. Later on the group was joined by the young history professor Granovsky, whose lectures created a sensation in the early forties. With this Granovsky Turgenev became acquainted in 1835 at the University of St. Petersburg.

We find that during this period, for about three years (1833-1836), Turgenev came under the influence of Byron and Shakespeare. He learned English and tried to read *Othello, Hamlet,* and *King Lear.* The picture of Byron's Manfred, with his gloomy protest and negation, and that of Shakespeare's Hamlet, with his profound doubt, continually haunted him.

In October 1837 Turgenev took his university degree at St. Petersburg. In May of the following year he went to Berlin. There he attended university courses in philosophy with Professor Werder and heard lectures in philology and history. Granovsky and Stankevich were also there.

Just what was the intellectual atmosphere in Russia at this time?

During the early decades of the nineteenth century the philosophy of Schelling and Hegel took strong hold of the intellectual youth. There sprang up in Moscow various circles, the purpose of the members of which was to familiarize themselves with German science. There was a desire for a broader acquaintance with Western ideals. Such concepts as *nation, national spirit, national destiny* became matters of close study. In the forties a democratic spirit swept over Europe and the younger generation of authors began to feel it their duty to teach and propagate definite social ideals and to become champions of the cause of liberty.

These young writers had developed an inquiring spirit and could not help noticing the vast abyss that lay between their theories and the dark reality about them. They felt how the iron traditions of the past left the nation chained to the ground, making all progress impossible. The consequence was that some developed a strain of skepticism. Others became absorbed in self analysis with a view of examining the new ideas that took hold of their minds. Still others turned pessimistic. Turgenev's impressionable nature was bound to catch the spirit of the day: indeed he was the first to express his interest in the lower strata in an effective manner.

In 1840 after a short stay in Russia and a trip to Italy he returned to Berlin where he remained about a year, living with Bakunin. Suggestions of his friendship with Bakunin we find in *Rudin*, in Lezhnev's reminiscences about his early association with Rudin[6] What attracted him so powerfully abroad? His letters and references to that period point to the fact that one reason was his dissatisfaction with the low status of learning in the Russian universities. Far more important motives were the desire to stay at a distance from the Lutovinov estate, from his mother's despotic rule, and the desire to postpone his entering the government service—something his mother very much insisted upon. Above all there was the desire to be at as great a distance as possible from the atmosphere of serfdom. In his "Literary Reminiscences" he says:

Each one of us felt that his land was great and plentiful, but that there was no order in it.

---

[6] Turgenev, *op. cit.*, IV, 395-96.

About myself I wish to say that I was aware of the disadvantages consequent upon my becoming alienated from my native land, and my tearing asunder the ties that were binding me to that environment amid which I grew up; but there was nothing else to be done. The status of landed proprietors to which I belonged and their exercising freely prerogatives over the serfs held out nothing to me that could keep me back. On the contrary, almost everything I saw about me used to provoke in me a feeling of indignation and disgust. I could not hesitate very long. Either it was necessary to submit and follow calmly the beaten track, or to turn away at once, to discard everything and everybody; even at the risk of losing much that was dear and near to my heart. And so I did. I plunged headfirst into the "German Sea" which was to cleanse me and give me new birth. When I emerged from its waves, I found myself a "Westerner" and such I have remained forever.[7]

His desire to stay at a distance from the Lutovinov estate helps explain his reluctance to continue an active correspondence with his mother, in spite of her imperious demands, in spite of her threats to flog the fine looking Nikolenka, the son of a serf, one whom Turgenev liked very much.

Having severed connection with his native *milieu* of noblemen favoring serfdom, Turgenev was trying to find friends and sympathizers among the intelligent noblemen of the "leader" type, among the *émigrés* who had become "useless" in their country of bonded slaves. He found many of this type among students. An echo of this mood of his we find in his story "Andrey Kolosov," the hero of which is a student who suffers from a certain undefinable dissatisfaction, a boredom he tries to escape.

Turgenev's intimacy with Stankevich ripened in 1840, in Rome. Stankevich, who possessed a profound knowledge of philosophy, rare reasoning powers, and marked aesthetic inclinations had also the faculty of reading deeply into people's hearts. The two friends used to meet daily. These meetings had a great influence upon Turgenev who was then only twenty-two and given much to hamletizing. Stankevich was an active enthusiast and his enthusiasm communicated itself to the young Turgenev. To what extent our writer idealized him one can see in "Andrey Kolosov," "Yakov Pasynkov" and in the

[7] *Ibid.*, X, 3.

character of Pekorsky in *Rudin*. "When I portrayed Pekorsky," says Turgenev "the image of Stankevich was before my eyes."[8] The death of Stankevich in July 1840 moved Turgenev most deeply.

In the same year his friendship with Bakunin developed. Turgenev conceived a warm attachment for one of his sisters, as his letters of the period indicated. To this friendship he ascribed great importance. He now became an ardent student and admirer of Hegel and espoused many of the views entertained by the Bakunins. His circle of friends widened and in 1841, when he was back in Moscow, he became more closely acquainted with Granovsky and with the Slavophiles, and Aksakovs, and also with Hertsen.

In the forties social and economic questions began to stir the minds of the intelligentsia more vigorously than hitherto. Turgenev came under their influence. When he was in the service of the Russian government, in the Department of the Interior, he handed in a report "A Few Remarks Concerning the Russian Economic Status and the Russian Peasantry."[9] Among other things he said:

All the Russian people are watching the acts of the government with a feeling of hopefulness and of certainty and are convinced that the change from the former patriarchal state of the Russian peasants and the Russian economic policy to a new and more constructive policy will yield favorable results.

In 1842 Turgenev met Byelinsky. During the four winters, from 1843 to 1846, they saw much of each other, having long discussions that lasted sometimes six hours. What were the subjects of these discussions? In his "Reminiscences" Turgenev says:

The subjects of our talks were mostly of an uncensored nature. They bore on ideals of science, of progress, of humanism, of civilization, in short, ideals of Westernism.

"The people" interest Turgenev very much in the forties. In "Razgovor" ("The Conversation,") the young man says:

> For you, my people
> I shall joyfully go forward—

---

[8] *Russkie Propilei* (St. Petersburg, 1916), III, 138.
[9] *Ibid.*, III, 89-100.

And once again shall spring up in my heart
A holy and brotherly love.[10]

In his poem "Tolpa" ("The Crowd,") we get a glimpse of his state of
mind at about 1846. The following is a paraphrase of a portion of
the poem:

Among the people I roam aimlessly, without
desire. Their amusements appear ridiculous to
me; still more ridiculous are to me my
sufferings! Of these sufferings the crowd takes
no note.

Characteristic is the following apostrophe to the crowd:

Thou art right, O Crowd!
Thou art great, and broad and as deep as the sea.
In your waves everything sinks: both the senseless
longings and the real grief. And thou are strong![11]

In his plays and tales of this period we find the evidence of
democratic notions appearing as casual remarks frequently woven
into the general plan of the story. These can be traced in his very
early productions. Thus, in *Carelessness* his earliest play (1843) we
find him defining life as the "Free development of all our powers."[12]
Or, referring to country conditions, the hero Zhazikov of *Bezdenezhye*
("Broke") (1844), says: There is one bad feature about the country
—the poverty and oppression which exist there will be quite disagree-
able to a man with my high ideals.[13]

In "Tri Portreta" ("Three Portraits") (1846)[14] his purpose is defined somewhat better. It is a story intended to show the inhumanity
and the feeling of irresponsibility of some of the landowners of the
day. Read by or to a peasant, it would have a tendency to arouse a
feeling of revolt against the landed aristocracy. Vasily Ivanovich
Luchinov, a libertine of about thirty, came from St. Petersburg to the
village of Luchinovka, to attempt to get some money from his father,

[10] Turgenev, *Yunosheskiya Stikhotvoreniya* (Ladyzhnikov Ed., 1920), p. 411.
[11] *Loc. cit.*
[12] Sochineniya, IX, 33; Mandell trans., p. 30.
[13] *Ibid.*, IX, 87; Mandell trans., p. 72.
[14] *Ibid.*, V, 96-132.

a close-fisted gentleman. He succeeded in persuading the old servant to give him the key from the money bags. When the father discovered it, a row took place. The son left. Shortly after that the father died.

Some two years later the son Vasily returns. He now seduces the ward Olga, who is to marry a kindhearted quiet gentleman, the owner of an estate in the neighborhood, Pavel Rogachev. This is only a beginning of the mischief he is brewing. He goes to Rogachev, who knows nothing about the matter, and acting out the faithful brother, who came to vindicate the honor of his sister, he demands an explanation. "Marry her at once, or fight," thunders Vasily. The rascal practically forces him to a duel, something the poor fellow was not prepared for. Of course, he is killed.

Vasily runs to his mother, saying, "Mother, honor has been avenged." He subsequently ends his existence in a wretched manner, having suffered a paralytic stroke that deprives him of speech. The story seems to have been written with a pen dipped in blood.

Sometimes we find merely a reference to the coarseness and lack of refinement of the wealthy landowner, as in *Nakhlyebnik* ("The Family Charge"), written in 1848.

As the forties reach their close, we find Turgenev becoming infected with the Western spirit of the approaching revolution of 1848. In 1847 he writes to Mme. Viardot[15] "Once the Social Revolution becomes a fact, then long live the New Literature." In 1849 we find him telling Mme. Viardot that he is reading and translating Saint Simon.

With the approach of the revolution of 1848 Turgenev gradually drifted away from Hegelianism. Berlin ceased to attract him. He went to Paris where social problems were seething and where subsequently Hertsen, Bakunin, and many of the German *émigrés* spent a considerable period. Prussian idealism began losing its hold on Turgenev's mind. He had to face reality now.

The attention of the intellectuals was now occupied with problems of social maladjustment, problems involving "the people." It was about this time that Turgenev writes in his "Reminiscences":

[15] Efimov, *Turgenev: Neizdannye pis'ma k gospozhe Viardo*, p. 29. Letter dated Dec. 25, 1847.

I could not breathe the air in an atmosphere that I hated. I had to be away from my enemy that I might attack him the more powerfully from a distance. In my eyes this enemy had well defined features and bore a definite name: my enemy bore the name of Serf-Laws. Against this enemy I have decided to fight till the very end and made a vow never to be reconciled to him. That was my Hannibal oath. I crossed to the West that I might fulfill my oath more effectively.[16]

We have already seen that his aversion to the Lutovinov estate contributed in no small measure to his leaving Russia. Later on his love for Pauline Viardot played, of course, a considerable part in his making Western Europe his domicile.

Our chapter on influences upon Turgenev would be hardly complete without a few words about his uncle, Nicolas Turgenev (1789-1871). The central ambition of this man's life was the amelioration of the condition of the masses. This thought was never absent from his mind. He was brooding over the theme long before the Decembrist movement in which he was interested. In his work *La Russie et les Russes* (1847), as well as other writings, this theme continually recurs and remains uppermost. He did not hesitate when a sacrifice of personal interest was required. All his works, his letters, in so far as they reflect his social and political interest, repeatedly impress us with the fact that outside of the ambition to see his country free, there was little else he desired.

In 1856, rumors reached him about projects on foot to soften the lot of the Russian peasant and we find the following remark in his notebook:

Today I was informed that on the day of coronation it is the intention of the emperor to free all the peasants born henceforth into a state of bondage. I could not believe that sacred news. In so confused a state of mind was I, that I could not collect my thoughts. In the afternoon I remained at home alone; tears streamed from my eyes and I wept aloud. I saw in my mind the newly-born infants coming into the world free, and not serfs.[17]

---

[16] Turgenev, *Sochineniya*, X, 3.

[17] Brodsky, *Turgenev i ego vremya*, p. 207.

Our author was thrown into his uncle's path at an early age and the almost life-long association of this fighter for freedom could not remain without its influence. On the question of peasant reforms, their ideas seemed to converge to the same points of agreement. In December, 1859 Ivan writes from St. Petersburg to his Uncle Nicolas:

Tout ce que je puis vous dire, c'est que la grande affaire de l'emancipation marche bien, que le général Rostovtseff[18] jouit toujours de la pleine confiance de l'Empereur et qu'il y a tout lieu de croire que la publication de l'uckase aura lieu au printemps. Les réformes judiciaires ne se feront pas non plus longtemps attendre, d'après des renseignements certains.[19]

Nicolas Turgenev was known to have done much towards improving the lot of the peasants under Alexander I, among whose advisers he was for some time. Later on he became mixed up with the Decembrist movement. After their failure to gain a constitutional government for Russia, he succeeded in escaping the vengeance of Nicholas I by fleeing to France. It was here that he published *La Russie et les Russes,* considered as the first vindication of the Russian revolution.

During the period of his stay in Berlin University, Turgenev visited his uncle now and then. It is probable that the latter initiated him into the ideas of liberty that influenced our author for the remaining period of his life.

Among Turgenev's associations the relation with the brilliant journalist Alexander Hertsen could not be without effects. Turgenev became one of the most active contributors to his *Kolokol,* a revolutionary paper started by Hertsen in London. This paper had great influence in Russia. The correspondence with Hertsen shows that Turgenev was one of the most clear-sighted political thinkers of the time. Students of modern history find Turgenev's judgment of the soundest and most correct.

It is only natural that his strong love of liberty and his radical

[18] General Rostovtseff, well known in his time as one of the most active workers for the liberation of the serf.
[19] Brodsky, *op. cit.,* p. 215.

views should have colored Turgenev's literary work. Indeed there is hardly one of his major works that fails to bear the stamp of his individuality. By many he is considered the standard-bearer and inspirer of liberal thinking Russia. Looked at from a certain point of view, the characters in his novels are living men and women in whom his ideas and aspirations are embodied in concrete form. From one point of view, his novels may be looked upon as an intellectual history of a very interesting period in the evolution of modern Russia.

Chapter III

A SPORTSMAN'S SKETCHES: THE VOICE UNDER COVER

The years 1847-1851 were years of strenuous literary activity for Turgenev. A number of the sketches in the *Sportsman's Diary* were written during this period. The first eight were printed in 1847. Most of these and the later ones appeared in the *Sovremyennik* ("Contemporary") between 1847-1851. The following, however, appeared at a much later period: "Zhivya Moshchi" ("The Living Relics") (1874), "Stuchit" ("One Knocks") (1875). All these sketches are unified by the sameness of theme. In all of them one sees the face of his bitterest enemy, the Serf Law, and the main hero is the Serf.

Contrary to Gogol, who caricatures the peasant, Turgenev takes his characters directly from life and gives us true portraits, much idealized, to be sure. They are thinking beings, feeling profoundly and able to give utterance to their emotions in their own individual manner. The innocent titles, the absence of high-flown rhetoric, and the fact that as they appeared, one by one, they received little publicity, saved them from the censor's ax. Only when they appeared together did the cumulative impressions produce a totally different effect upon the reading public. One immediately saw a protest against the inhuman system of oppression of those whom nature endowed with powers of mind and heart that made them the equal of their oppressors. In fact, in all these stories the master is distinctly inferior to the slave, both intellectually and emotionally. The synthesis of all the sketches resolved itself into an indictment of the Serf Law. In choosing his type for the master, Turgenev did not necessarily take the cruel one, but one who would represent the average. A good example is furnished by the "Dva Pomyestshika" ("Two Landowners").[1] This renders the picture of serf-oppression more vivid and more convincing.

---

[1] Turgenev, *Polnoye sobraniye sochinenii* I, 199.

Turgenev was not the only writer whom the country and the peasant interested. In 1845-1846 Nekrasov wrote his verses about peasant life; Grigorovich wrote his *Derevnia* ("Village") in 1846, and *Anton Goremyka* in 1847; Dostoyevsky wrote his *Poor People* in 1845, and Hertsen his *Soroka-Vorovka* in 1848. The peasant was coming in for his share in literature about this time. Turgenev was not unaware of these works. In December of 1847 he wrote "I have come across a remarkable novel of a certain Grigorovich."[2]

It is very probable that George Sand's *Country Stories* had an influence on Turgenev's technique in the descriptive portion of the sketches. While in Courtavenal he read these with eagerness. Between 1844 and 1850 George Sand wrote *Jeanne* (1845); *La Mare au Diable* (1846); *La Petite Fadette* (1849); *François le Champi* (1850). All these works are permeated with descriptions of country life and country scenery. Turgenev's keen eye could not fail to notice these. We find him writing his impressions to Pauline Viardot: "She writes simply, truthfully, and in a captivating manner. That woman has the talent to convey the most elusive impressions firmly, and clearly."[3] The social tendencies of George Sand's works could not have remained without a certain influence on Turgenev. As late as 1876 we find him writing to Gustave Flaubert: "Russian society belongs to those upon whom Mme. Sand had the greatest influence."[4] The Russian society referred to is the society of the forties and writers like Byelinsky, with his social tendencies; Hertsen, the author of *Kto Vinovat?* ("Who is Guilty?"); Druzhinin (*Polinka Saks*); Grigorovich (*Anton Goremyka*); Dostoyevsky (*Poor People*); Saltykov-Shchedrin, and Turgenev himself.

On March 14, 1848 Tsar Nicholas I issued a manifesto with an appeal to all Russian subjects to fight against revolt and anarchy that had its rise in France. Turgenev was summoned by his mother to come to Spasskoye, but he remained in Paris which was hot with social revolt. In May 1850 he was still in Paris. There were very few days

---

[2] Letter to Mme. Viardot, Jan. 17, 1848. (Quoted from L'vov-Rogachevsky, *Turgenev, Zhizn' i Tvorchestvo*, p. 98.)   [3] *Loc. cit.*

[4] Letter dated June 18, 1876. Turgenev's letters to Mme. Viardot and his French friends (Halperine-Kaminsky Collection), p. 82.

then, when he failed to think of his duty toward Russia. We find him writing to Mme. Viardot:[5]

I am as happy as a child to find myself here. I have been to say "How d' you do" to all the places I said good-bye to before going away. Russia must wait, with its vast and sombre countenance, motionless and veiled like the sphinx of Oedipus. She will swallow me up later on. I seem to see her large inert gaze fixed upon me, with a dreary scrutiny of eyes of stone. Never mind, sphinx, I shall return to thee, and thou mayest devour me at thine ease. I shall return to thy steppes!

However, in July he went to Russia to see his mother. During the interview sharp words passed and the son unburdened his heart, pointing out among other things his mother's cruel relation to the serfs. She drove him out. The result of the ten days' stay was a complete break between mother and son. A few months later the mother died. Turgenev at once freed all his serfs. Some of them preferred to remain quit-rent tenants. In selling the land he would allow one-fifth to the peasant without charge, and on the main estate a considerable quantity of the land was distributed entirely free.[6] The condition of Russia was preying more and more upon his mind during the fifties. Hereafter it was going to be his life's problem to solve the Riddle of Russia.

We have already noted that in 1850 Turgenev was in Russia, where he stayed for a brief period. That period was perhaps one of the darkest in Russia's history, for it lay then under the heel of one of its most extreme autocrats Nicholas I, who had to assist him a servile press, and a bureaucratic régime forced into complete subservience. Philosophy was a forbidden subject in schools and universities. Historical publications were placed under strict censorship. No history of the seventeenth or eighteenth century was allowed to be taught in any form whatsoever. Anyenkov, Turgenev's friend and adviser says about these days:

The fear of the government of a possible revolution, terror within partly engendered by that fear, persecution of the press, reenforcement of the police force, suspicion, repressive measures without limit and, appar-

---

[5] May 16, 1850 (Halperine Kaminsky Collection).
[6] Brodsky, *Turgenev i ego vremya*, p. 236.

ently, without any need—are some of the facts of the day. The peasant question that had just about been brought before the public was set aside. Saltykov is in prison for one of his novels. Upon the scene appears Buturlin with his hatred of word, thought and freedom and his preaching of unconditional obedience, silence, and discipline. Unwonted theories of education are becoming a foundation for the perversion of minds, characters and nature.[7]

If in addition we take into consideration the immense excitement that was caused by the appearance abroad, in 1850, of a French translation of Hertsen's "About the Development of Revolutionary Ideas in Russia," then we shall readily see that Turgenev hardly chose a propitious occasion to come to Russia. The atmosphere was most stifling to one who had but recently been an eye witness of the Social Revolution in France. Even before his arrival the army of censors lined up ready for their prey.

In 1849 the censorship forbade the printing of his play *Nakhlyebnik* ("The Boarder"), on the ground that the episodes represented the Russian nobleman in an unfavorable light. In 1850 they forbade the printing of his comedy *Zavtrak u predvoditelya* ("Breakfast at the Chairman's"), although it had already been acted before. The only thing that may have possibly offended them was a passing reflection on the inefficiency of the police.[8] Another comedy, *The Student*, the subject of which is the love rivalry between a mature married woman and a young girl, was written in 1849-1850. It could not appear until 1855, and then in a very mutilated form and with a changed name: *A Month in the Country*—all to satisfy the requirement of the censors. A democratic tendency is clearly apparent in certain portions of the play, such as Mme. Islayeva's discussion with the teacher Byelyayev about her boy's education. She would have him grow up in freedom. Oppression and suppression make for unhappiness.[9]

On February 21st Gogol died. Turgenev wrote an obituary notice in the *St. Petersburg News* in which he referred to Gogol as "the great." Count Musin-Pushkin, who was in charge of the St. Peters-

[7] P. I. Anenkov, *Literaturnye Vospominaniya*, p. 43.

[8] *Sochineniya*, IX, 374; M. S. Mandell, *The Plays of Ivan S. Turgenev*, p. 313.   [9] *Sochineniya*, IX, 443; Mandell trans., p. 370.

burg educational zone, forbade the printing of this epithet. Turgenev's friends, however, had the notice reprinted in the *Moscow News,* including the forbidden epithet. This led to the author's arrest on April 16. A month later he was ordered to his village estate where he was to be under police inspection.

In his former writings he had already given sufficient provocation to the administrative authorities and they regarded his thoughts too dangerous to be given circulation. His liberal views were already too well known and greater frankness was feared. So, although the article was practically harmless, the government was glad to seize upon it as a pretense for silencing him. Referring to his arrest in his writing to Mme. Viardot, he says: "The authorities wished to put an end to all that was being said about Gogol's death, and they were not sorry, at the same time to put a stopper on my literary activity."[10] In the same letter he speaks of his interest in the Russian people. "I shall go on with my studies of the Russian people, the strangest, the most astonishing people on the face of the earth."

In 1853 he began sending petitions to be allowed to leave for St. Petersburg. In November of that year the desired permission was granted. In December we find him in St. Petersburg writing his famous "Mumu." After many alterations this story appeared, in 1854 in *Sovremyennik* ("Contemporary"), in the March number. It is a bitter page reproduced from scattered fragments of his autobiography. The story is as powerful as any of the most impressive tales in *The Sportsman's Sketches* and suggests the desolate condition of the serf. Though not of the lachrymose type, the story is full of pathos. There is a pent-up bitterness set loose in the description of the calmness and indifference with which the mistress of the household deals out her acts of tyranny. In this mistress we recognize his own mother reigning with absolute power on her domain.

"Mumu" is perhaps the most powerful denunciation that came from Turgenev's pen. It symbolizes the desolate condition of the Russian muzhik. In this apparently simple story of a serf's sacrificing his favorite dog, the writer seems to have dipped deep into the fountains of sympathy with the unfortunate. There is almost something Satanic in his dealing with the description of the various

[10] Letter of May 13, 1852. (Helperine-Kaminsky Collection.)

phases of tyranny in the mistress' household. The character of the deaf-mute serf Gerasim evidently appealed tremendously to our writer, as representative of the inarticulate suffering of millions.

Turgenev must have been burning with the fire of resentment against his enemy Serfdom when he wrote this story. But he had the example upon his mother's manor. The story was taken from life. There was a serf Andrey, whom Turgenev's mother noticed working in the field while making a tour of inspection through her domain. Struck by his colossal stature she stopped the carriage and ordered him to be brought to her. He proved to be a deaf-mute. He interested her much at the moment and she had him enroll among her servants. As in the story he was compelled to destroy a little dog Mumu, upon which all his affections had been concentrated.

There is no doubt that Turgenev could recall many such incidents of cruelty in his own home. He must have been impressed by the silent endurance of the peasant, his good qualities and boundless patience. Andrey became the symbol of dumb suffering peasantry. The impressions of his youth came back to him even later in old age. He could never forget his mother's playing with human lives with less concern than a child does with its toys. By the friends of the government the publication "Mumu" was considered one of the most serious slips of the censor, for in it is revealed an unfavorable applications of a landowner's powers to the bonded peasant. This story was only one of the first steps. What he was particularly anxious about was to see a separate edition of *The Sportsman's Sketches*, which he planned in two volumes.

As we noted before,[11] the sketches had already appeared separately, most of them in the *Contemporary*. In May of 1852, the censorship committee had under its investigation the manuscript of the sketches to be included in both volumes. Comparisons were made between the revised manuscript and the previous texts. The censor's report indicates (1) that a few words were added here and there for the sake of clearness and forcefulness, (2) that certain phrases were added for the sake of completeness, definiteness, and of beauty in descriptive passages. The report also points out the portions that had appeared in the *Contemporary*, but were omitted in the manuscript.

[11] See p. 23 of this work.

Permission was granted for the printing, but further investigation led Prince Shirinsky-Shakhmatov, minister of Public Education, to require the dismissal of the censor, Prince L'vov, for negligence in allowing the work to pass. In his report to Tsar Nicholas I, he said:

A considerable number of the passages have a tendency to degrade the land owners who are generally represented either as caricatures or in a way prejudicial to their honor. The spread of such unfavorable opinions regarding the landed gentry will no doubt contribute to a disrespectful attitude toward the nobility on the part of readers.

However, the permission was not retracted, but for the immediate future a reprint of the work was forbidden. After such hints one might well understand that Turgenev had to use extreme precaution in setting forth his views, so as not to offend the censors.

The series of sketches appeared in its combined form in 1855 under a rather misleading title *Zapiski Okhotnika* ("The Notes of a Hunter") in order to evade the suspicion of the censorship. A number of the sketches in which the cruelty of the masters is described were undoubtedly suggested to Turgenev by actual occurrences in his mother's household. A document has been preserved in which reference is made to the cruelty of one of the Lutovinov ancestors, perhaps an uncle to Turgenev's mother. The story must have furnished material for "The Peasant-Proprietor Ovsyanikov" as well as for the dramatic narrative, "Three Portraits." The document consists of notes written by Bakarev, who had lived in the province of Orel as architect.[12]

Considered one by one these sketches are characterized by simplicity, sincerity, the absence of satirical element, freedom from surprises and sensations: and yet, according to the opinion of some critics, they gave a decided blow to serfdom. To write about the atrocities in an out-and-out fashion would make the author's purpose too apparent. One had to be on guard against that all along. These atrocities are suggested in some, to be sure. But on the whole, the method is to give us life-portraits of living beings, sensible, and able to reason. The author does by no means give us any idealized picture of the Russian peasant, but such as he knew him to be.

[12] Brodsky, *Turgenev i ego Vremya*, p. 316.

They are bent under the yoke of serfdom at the hands of the serf-owners who led a mean and shallow existence. The life of the peasant as he lived in the earlier years of the nineteenth century is depicted in a lucid manner and the humble Russian toiler is put before the reader at close range. Contrast is furnished by sketches of the overseer, the landed proprietor, and representatives of other intermediate classes.

The facts he disclosed came as a revelation and struck a responsive chord. Writers before him spoke of the peasant in a light, humorous vein or in an idealized fashion making him the hero amid pastoral scenes. The dark side, the utter misery, the helpless condition, tragic in the extreme, were first brought to light by Turgenev. The immediate influence of these sketches was to impress the reader with the sense of wrong done by the system. Their social influence can hardly be overestimated. They aroused contempt for the serf-owner who abused the privileges vested in him. On the other hand, they gave rise to strong sympathy for a class of down-trodden beings who were shown to be superior to their masters in nobility of character.

In the first sketch "Khor and Kalinich" of the edition of 1855 there is hardly any direct suggestion of abuses at the hands of the serf-owning class. On the contrary, one gets the impression that the peasant's economic welfare and moral well-being can be traced more readily to his subjective state and to his ability to make the most of his circumstances. The peasant of Kaluga province is contrasted with that of the Orel province. The first is represented by Khor, the second by Kalinich. The former can readily adapt himself to his environment, the other cannot. Khor is not devoid of enterprising ability. Some twenty-five years back his hut had burned down. He applied to his master for the permission to lease a spot on a bit of marshy ground, apparently worthless. He got it at fifty rubles per year rental, with exemptions from any other money obligation. Since that time he has flourished marvelously and has even accumulated some money. There is no sign of marshy ground now. One sees there an agreeable and neat-looking wooden house. He has six sons, each one a giant, each one with a suggestion of the father's shrewdness.

The peasant has his prejudices. Among these, the attitude toward women is significant. To Khor they are foolish folk. Still he would rather see his son Fedya married. "The peasant woman is a laborer and the peasant's servant," he says by way of impressing his son.[13] The notion of domineering became so ingrained both in the high and the low, that no sooner would the serf be in a position to lord it over some one else, than he would do so with a vengeance.

Kalinich is a sort of village Hamlet. He has no initiative, has no practical turn of mind, but is a dreamer. He can only serve as another's tool. So he would accompany his master on his daily hunting trip, carry his supply bag, sometimes his gun, and do similar tasks. Kalinich is nearer to nature, Khor nearer to men. Turgenev treats the weaker of the two characters, Kalinich, with a motherly tenderness. "I admired his face for a long time, his gentle face, as clear as the evening sky,"[14] he says in describing the bearded peasant.

This first sketch in the collection is a good example of Turgenev's treatment of the serf problem, and of his artistically "evasive" method. The offhand reader feels only the author's loving treatment of his characters. But back of that, in a chance suggestive remark here and there, one is conscious of the author's purpose to expose the serf-owners in an unfavorable light. Sometimes it is only a line. In a by-the-way manner he will mention that the landowner Polutykin had a lawsuit with his neighbor who had flogged[15] one of his peasant women.

The sarcastic and well-to-do Khor likes to poke fun at his friend Kalinich.

"Why does not your master get you a pair of boots?" he asks Kalinich. "You leave my master in peace. What do I need boots for? I am only a peasant!"

"Well, so am I. However, look." Saying these words he lifts his foot to show his boots.

"Ekh! you are not one of us!"

"If he at least gave you for foot cloths! You go hunting with him almost daily."

"Well, he does. Last year he allowed me a ten copeck coin."

Just think of Polutykin's generosity![16]

[13] *Sochineniya*, I, 9. Garnett trans., p. 11.
[14] *Sochineniya*, I, 6.   [15] *Ibid.*, I, 7.
[16] *Ibid.*, I, 14.

So universal and common were the abuses practiced by the serf-owners, so little occasion was there for the perpetrators to fear the hand of justice that the average serf-owner did not even realize that there can be a question as to the moral side of his acts. That is best shown by Turgenev in his second sketch entitled "Ermolai and the Miller's Wife."

Zvyerkov (derived from *Zvyer'*—an animal) is very much put out by a case of ingratitude he cannot forget. One day, driving through his estate he noticed a comely child, a girl. It would be a nice idea to bring up that girl to be a kitchen-maid. The idea appealed to his wife, who was far from being kind-hearted, but whom her husband considered the gentlest creature in the world. The parents had not the courage to refuse. The girl's crying was heeded very little. She remained in the household for some ten years when one day she showed her "ungratefulness" by daring to ask permission to marry the man she loved.

"I must admit that I was astonished," says Zvyerkov.
"Do you know, you fool, that your mistress has no other personal maid?"
"I shall serve her as I did before."
"Nonsense! your mistress does not care to keep any married servants."
"Malanya can take my place."
"No discussions, please!"[17]

The poor girl made a second appeal half a year later. She was again refused. When a few months after that his wife brought to his attention that what was to be feared did happen, the girl was removed from the household to join the lot of the common serfs. Her lover was turned over to the military authorities, to serve as soldier. Later on, the miller bought her freedom and married her. She pined away in misery.

When we turn to the third sketch "The Raspberry Spring"[18] we find a character, Stepushka, intended to show to what degree of self-debasement the conditions of serfdom can bring an individual. His wretched state is first suggested by his outward appearance: small, thin, in a patched sort of coat, hatless. What little amount of vital energy he possessed was being exploited by anyone he came

[17] *Ibid.*, I, 27.   [18] *Ibid.*, I, 63.

across. He was, for instance, considered good enough to assist in fishing, by holding the can of worms. Characteristic is the author's remark, when he speaks of the removal of the household where Stepushka had previously found shelter. That was after a fire on the Shumikhino estate. The landholders had decided to change residence. Except for Mitrofan and his family, and Gerasim, "no one" was left on the estate, for Stepushka "could not in general, be considered as a human being." He even had no "past." In a census count they hardly thought it worth while to include him. Everyone refused to notice him.

Formerly, on holidays, when the serfs would line up before their master, bow to him and go over to kiss his hand, Stepushka would stand in some obscure spot, trying to look as small as possible. No one expected those civilities of him, for no one thought of his presence. He would, of course, miss the usual treat of a glass of wine and some cake, unless some kind soul happened to thrust into his hand a piece that some one left unfinished.

This sketch offers another excellent example of Turgenev's indirect method of handling his problem. No one is blamed, no invectives are used. The reader is allowed to draw his own conclusion as to the sort of characters that were a product of the serf system.

And so Turgenev continues, without any pre-arranged plan, to point out one phase or another of the conditions of the times. In "L'gov" he introduces a downtrodden individual Suchok (from *Suk* —a twig), a type smiliar to Stepushka, whose acquaintance we made in the "Raspberry Spring." He appears barefoot, in tatters, unkempt —in the greatest degree of shabbiness imaginable. If there ever was any will in the man, the last vestige of it was crushed. In none of Turgenev's works do we find so forlorn and boneless an individual. So used has this man of sixty become to his wretched state that he is not even conscious of the wrong that has been done to him. Just now he has been assigned the task of being in charge of the fish— in a fishless pond. The previous owner had him fill the post of driver. Some six years he was cook. Before that, "actor" and shoemaker. All these changes of status were incident to the change of proprietors upon the estate to which he belonged.

Has he been married? No. The proprietress did not permit him to marry. Suchok feels no resentment. He is conscious of no wrong done to him. He has a ready excuse for his masters.

"Do you receive any pay?" asks Ermolai.

"Pay?—what for—pay?!—Eatables are given—glory to God, for that! I am quite satisfied. May God prolong my mistress' years!

One of the most loving characters we find is Kasyan (described in a subsequent sketch). The hunter, having had some trouble with his wagon because of a broken wheel, turned to the nearest hut, in the hope of finding some help. There, lying on the ground of a neglected courtyard, near a dilapidated shanty, he found Kasyan, a dwarf-like creature. "Is it not sinful to kill God's innocent creatures?" is the reproachful remark with which he greets the guest.

Kasyan is a peculiar fellow. His philosophy is that we must not kill birds. It is their right to live till it pleases Death to take them. However, he likes to hunt nightingales. He does not kill them. He traps them. He does it to give human beings pleasure. He says one must not torture them. Does he sell them? No; he gives them away to kind people. God rules human destiny, says Kasyan. Whomever God will not favor, him the same sun will not warm and him bread will not feed. Kasyan is a primitive soul enjoying the poetry of nature. His unsophisticated mind takes delight in the basking rays of the sun, in the growing of the grass, in the running of the brook, in the chirping of the birds. He sees in all that the generous hand of God. He is a philosopher without suspecting it.

The absolute futility of the peasant's attempt to obtain any justice by appeal to law is shown in "The Bailiff" and "The Office." When Arkady Pavlich Pyenochkin has corporal punishment administered to his subjects, it is done "for their good." He has spent some time in the West and brought, as the results of Western "culture," the outward polish without the inward refinement that should go with it. Though he will address his butler as "my dear" it will not prevent him from having the unfortunate fellow flogged for having forgotten to warm his wine.[19] He is the terror of all the serfs in the village. Behind his quiet manners the peasants feel the merciless despot. The bailiff of his village is worthy of his master. He rules with a tyrannous hand every inch of his little kingdom.

[19] *Sochineniya*, I, 153.

Arkady Pavlich went upon an inspection tour one day. One of the peasants gathered sufficient courage to complain against the bailiff, who pressed two of his sons into military service and was about to send the third one off. "He is drunk," explained the bailiff.[20] The matter was considered settled. Nothing but regret for having dared to complain was left to the poor peasant.

Again, in "The Office" when Pavel, one of the serfs, wished to marry a serf girl, the chief office clerk did not relish the idea. Though a married man in the fifties, he finds her worth his attention—for a passing flirtation. He used his influence to cast disfavor upon the poor girl. Of course, the mistress did not give her consent to the marriage. A row took place in the office, and Pavel, threw the clerk to the ground. The final upshot of the matter was that the girl was sent away to a different locality.

This absolute control of the love fortunes of the poor serfs by their masters is a topic that Turgenev likes to refer to frequently in his *Sketches*. It is developed in greater detail in "Petr Petrovich Karatayev." Karatayev is a small merchant who is in love with one of the kitchen maids. The mistress, a sour old maid, will not consent to the marriage, for she took it into her head to find a husband for a lady-companion of hers, another superannuated damsel. Karatayev seemed to her the man suitable to fill the post of honor. Karatayev is willing to pay a good sum to buy the girl's freedom. The mistress will not hear of it. "Can it be Matrona is so necessary to you?" asked Karatayev. "No," said she, "she is not necessary." "Then why won't you part with her and allow her to me?" "Because I don't choose to. I have already given my orders: she is being sent to a village in the steppes."[21] After sufficient persuasion the girl is induced to elope. She is upon Karatayev's estate until discovered. He patches the matter up with the bailiff by bribing him generously. Some time passes until one day she is seen driving by her mistress. The latter is desperate and will now have her back at any price. For some weeks the girl remains in hiding. Finally realizing how much trouble she has been causing, she decides to give herself up. Karatayev takes to drinking.

Of the twenty-two sketches that appeared in the first collected

[20] *Ibid.*, I, 163.   [21] *Ibid.*, I, 287.

edition, those analyzed above are perhaps the only ones that deal with the relations between the serf-owner and serf, between the oppressor and the oppressed. This alone could not be responsible for the great success of the book in hastening peasant reforms. For, it must be said, that Turgenev was by no means the first one to touch on that question. In 1846 Grigorovich wrote the novel, *The Village,* in which the wretched life of the serfs was painted in appealing colors. It marked the new direction in which social ideas were moving. Nevertheless, it is held that Turgenev's *Sketches* have contributed toward the Reforms more than any other literary work.

In the fifties these ideas gained momentum. One begins to notice a change of attitude toward the serf even among serf-owners. This change is hinted at partly in "The Peasant Proprietor Ovsyanikov," where we are told that a milder class of land-owners has succeeded the despotic old type. His stories bring to light the condition of the serfs and their attitude toward their masters. When the neighboring estate changed hands years ago the new master happened to be a young man who came from a big town, one who possessed a certain refinement of character. He attempted to treat the muzhiks more humanly, would tell them "Good morning," and in his actions imply that he considered them his equal. The peasants, however, refused to take him seriously, and feared him the more for it, thinking that there were malicious motives back of his actions. They had been treated like slaves so long that any different attitude on the part of their superiors appeared to them unnatural.

"Might makes right," says Ovsyanikov ready to speak of another form of abuse. A powerful neighbor appropriated part of his father's estate. When the latter made an attempt to hand a petition to the court, nothing came of it. Furthermore, the powerful neighbor had him brought over and flogged, forcing from him a promise that he would not press the case at court. It is interesting to compare some of these views with those suggested by Griboyedov. His *Gore ot Uma* ("Intelligence comes to Grief,") indicates an influx of Western ideas into Russia and foreshadows the conflict between Westerners and Slavophiles.

Not merely the subject-matter but the artistic manner in which Turgenev mirrored the struggles between a world of craft and greed and the appealing humbleness of suffering beings explains the secret of the success that the *Sketches* had. Sometimes there is no reference made at all to the relation of serf and serf-owner, as in "Lebedyan" "Death," "The Singers," "The Rattling of Wheels." They portray with a sympathetic pen the local life and social conditions and are truthful studies of the better side of the peasant's nature. The humble Russian toiler is put before the reader in his daily habits and as he lived in the earlier years of the nineteenth century. These serve as contrasts to such sketches as "The Bailiff," "The Office," "Petr Petrovich Karatayev," representing the landed proprietor at his worst.

In "Lebedyan" we merely see the bustle and stir of a horse-fair in a small country town, written apparently without particular intention to expose any special abuses.

"The Tryst" introduces us to the heroine Akulina who can suffer from slighted love no less than the grand ladies of the fashionable salon. We cannot forget the meeting with her conceited lover, the pampered valet Viktor. Our sympathy for the girl is accentuated by the author's marvelous treatment of the background scenery.

In "Death" we are shown how, in the face of death, the peasant's courage rises to sublimity. He dies coolly, simply, as though he were performing a solemn rite. When Maksim is crushed by a tree and has only a few minutes to live, he is concerned about his money going to his wife—*after deducting what he owes to others*. Or the case of the peasant who was injured in the fire and awaiting his death quietly, philosophically. Or, again, Vasily, who will not stay at the hospital, for he must be at home to set things right, in case he dies. "It makes no difference where one dies!" "The Russians die in a wonderful way,"[22] are the words with which the sketch concludes.

To bring the heroic qualities of the peasant into stronger relief, we have, on the other hand the serf-owner, sketched in a manner that makes us feel more than once that the serf is the better of the two. To be sure, we see the sign of western civilization on Pyenochkin's estate ("The Bailiff"). His farming agent Sofron sees to it that the village Sheplova can show a set of tidy farm buildings and thresh-

[22] *Sochineniya*, I, 255.

ing floors and rich hempfields. But the sharp, sweet-tongued fellow gets his share of it, and that at the expense of the poor peasants he exploits. He feels secure, for he has behind him the implicit confidence of his polished master who has only words of reprimand for the poor victims of his bailiff's greed, if they dare to complain. Such lack of discipline must not occur on *his* farm.

Whether these simple children of the soil be good or bad, they may be bought and sold, like any other commodity. How eloquently, in some half-dozen lines, does Turgenev sketch the bargaining for the possession of a serf girl! ("Karatayev").[23]

That these children of the steppes can feel the refined influences of music no less than the cultured Westerner, is the message of "The Singers." Yashka is a consumptive looking fellow. "What chance does he stand against me?" thinks the booth-keeper from Zhizdry. The tavern loungers are their critical audience. But they can feel! Their emotions swell with the rhythmical movements of the singer's voice. They are real human beings, an appeal to whose emotions will not fall on barren ground. And as to the singer himself:

He sang, utterly forgetful of his rival and all of us; he seemed supported, as a bold swimmer by the waves, by our silent passionate sympathy. He sang and in every sound of his voice one seemed to feel something of breath and space, as though the familiar steppes were unfolding before our eyes and stretching away into endless distance. I felt the tears gathering in my bosom and rising to my eyes; suddenly I was struck by dull smothered sobs. . . . I looked round—the innkeeper's wife was weeping. The humble peasant was sobbing softly in the corner and shaking his head with a plaintive murmur; and on the iron visage of the Wild Master, from under his overhanging brows there slowly rolled a heavy tear; the booth-keeper raised his clenched fists to his brow, and did not stir. . . . I don't know how the general emotion would have ended, if Yakov had not suddenly come to a full stop on a high, exceptionally shrill note, as though his voice had broken. No one called out or even stirred. Every one seemed to be waiting to see whether he was not going to sing more; but he opened his eyes as though wondering at our silence, looked around at all of us, and saw that the victory was his.

"Yasha," said the Wild Master, laying his hand on his shoulder, and he could say no more.

---

[23] *Ibid.*, I, 287.

We stood, as it were, petrified. The book-keeper softly rose and went up to Yakov. "You—yours, you've won," he articulated at last with an effort, and rushed out of the room.[24]

It has been said that Turgenev's *Sketches* added more to the campaign for the liberation of the serfs than all the political activities of the progressive faction combined. Even if this be only partly true, Turgenev performed a great service for suffering humanity. His purpose was to show that the Russian peasant is not devoid of the finer human qualities that the representatives of those classes who held him in bondage prided themselves upon. In Turgenev's sketches he appears in many respects better than his masters. In our age of psychologic realism this may be obvious, but it was not so in Turgenev's day. When Arina asks permission to be married to the man she loves, Zvyerkov, her master, cannot admit the possibility that feelings that move the "noble," element of society should find a place in *her* heart."[25]

It gradually entered the minds even of those hardheaded land owners that the peasants so artistically described by the pen of a genius, though simple men and women, were beings whose hearts were moved by the same emotions, whose souls were craving for the same truth, beauty, and good, as the upper classes. An innocent sketch like "The Singers" reveals that they are not devoid of artistic emotions, that their critical sense, as applied to music, can compare with those whose tastes have been trained.

Although it is only in some of the sketches that the peasant's misery is suggested, and that, too, in a casual way, we, nevertheless, get a complete representation of their miseries and their few joys. The treatment of the miller's wife, the characters of Stepushka and Suchkov, though portrayed economically in some dozen lines, give us an insight into the boundless wretchedness of these unhappy folk. And yet we must love them when we get a glimpse into the simple souls of such as Kasyan, which rise to lofty heights in their unconscious practical philosophy. We get an insight into the way their beliefs take root. They are only superstitions, but science never found its place among them and imagination took the place of scientific ob-

[24] *Ibid.*, I, 275.
[25] "Ermolai and the Miller's Wife," see p. 32 of this work.

servation and popular synthesis the place of logical deductions. That is what we note in "Byezhin Meadow." In spite of these superstitions, we are won over to the side of these simple folk, because of their boundless patience and the tenderness of their heart.

A tinge of gloom is always present in Turgenev's peasants. Delicately as it is suggested, its effect is so powerful that we no longer marvel at the opinion that has become so universally held that *The Sportsman's Sketches* did more to bring about the abolition of serfdom than did any uprising or political measure.

Few other Russian writers were better equipped to describe the joys and sorrows of their nation. Having been born in the province of Orel, whose inhabitants are perhaps far better representatives of the Russian lower classes than those of any other province, he was peculiarly well fitted for his task. There he was able to watch for many years at close quarters the manifestations of national life. If it be pointed out that his having written most of his works abroad was likely to result in introducing a false note here and there, one may offset this by the fact that he was thereby able to reproduce with an unprejudiced mind the impressions treasured up in his youth and frequently verified by keen observation. It is conceded that there are very few works that are more thoroughly Russian than are the works of Turgenev. It is thus that he was able to write his sketches, while only going at odd times back to his native country. His separation from his country only served to intensify his love for it.

In his "Literary Reminiscences" Turgenev explains his feelings with regard to practices in his country. They embittered him so that he found it impossible to stay there.

The existing state of things, the whole social fabric, and particularly the class to which I belonged—the class of landlords and serf owners— held out no inducement which could have kept me in my own country. On the contrary, almost everything that I saw about me distressed me, filled me with indignation and scorn. I could not remain undecided for long. I had either to submit, to walk meekly in the common rut, or tear myself away with one wrench, casting off everything and everybody at the risk of losing many who were near and dear to my heart. I chose the latter course.[26]

---

[26] *Sochineniya*, X, 3.

It is doubtful whether Turgenev could have written *The Sportsman's Sketches* had he remained at home. It was impossible for him, he said, to breathe the same air that gave life to everything he abhorred. He needed some draught of a more liberal European atmosphere.[27]

To this period refer also the stories "Perepiska" ("Correspondence") (1854), *Zatishye* ("A Quiet Backwater") (1854), "Yakov Pasynkov" (1855). They express the despair of the educated Russian. "We Russians," says Alexey Petrovich to his lady correspondent, "have set ourselves no other task in life but the cultivation of our own personality, and when we're children hardly grown-up we set to work to cultivate it, this luckless personality."[28] Our intellect does not bring us very far, he complains:

Receiving no definite guidance from without, with no real respect for anything, no strong belief in anything, we are free to make what we choose of ourselves . . . one can't expect every one to understand on the spot the uselessness of intellect "seething in vain activity" . . . and so we get again one monster the more in the world, one more of those worthless creatures in whom habits of self-consciousness distort the very striving for truth. We are psychologists. But our psychology is akin to pathology; our psychology is that subtle study of the laws of morbid condition and morbid development, with which healthy people have nothing to do.[29]

Characteristic is the remark from the girl's letter about the weak intellectuals: There are no heroes nowadays— . . . Great would be his power over her. . . . If he were a hero, he would fire her, would teach her to sacrifice herself, and all sacrifices would be easy to her![30]

By 1855 Turgenev finds himself ready to start upon the field of social novels of which the most epoch-making are: *Rudin* (1855); *A Nobleman's Nest* (1858); *On the Eve* (1859); *Fathers and Children* (1861); *Smoke* (1866); *Virgin Soil* (1876). These we shall take up in detail in the three following chapters.

[27] *Ibid.*, X, 3.
[28] *Ibid.*, VI, 102; Garnett trans., XIII, 283.
[29] *Ibid.*, VI, 102; Garnett trans., XIII, 284.
[30] *Ibid.*, VI, p. 106; Garnett trans., XIII, 288.

CHAPTER IV

ON THE EVE OF REFORM: RUDIN; A NOBLEMAN'S NEST; ON THE EVE

It is in his novels that Turgenev best expresses his views and attitude toward democracy. These deserve careful study, for, in general, it may be said that in no other country does literature occupy so influential a position as in Russia. One may venture a step further and say that nowhere else does it exercise so profound and so direct an influence upon the intellectual development of the younger generation.

There are very definite reasons why the past literature exercised such a tremendous influence. There was no open political life and, throughout the nineteenth century, with the exception of a few years at the time of the abolition of serfdom, the Russian people have never been called upon to take an active part in the framing of their country's institutions. The consequence has been that the best minds of the country have chosen literary forms for expressing their aspirations, their conception of national life, or their ideals. Among such minds Turgenev occupies the foremost rank and his novels give us for the period they cover, perhaps the best picture of the movement of the destiny of Russia.

In our treating of Turgenev's democratic ideas, his novels form a prominent part. They are not mere random stories dealing with a certain chance event that may come under the author's observation. They have a close connection and present to us certain intellectual types who have made a great impression on Russian readers, particularly so upon the younger generation. During the three decades covered by Turgenev's novels Russian society had undergone deep and rapid modifications. It was in a certain sense a 19th century "renaissance." Having cast off serfdom, Russian society was now awakening and rushing toward a richer and more progressive life. It is this awakening spirit that we shall attempt to trace.

There are no indications that Turgenev followed any preconceived plans. "A truly talented writer is the condensed expression of life itself,"[1] he wrote. But as soon as life brought under his sharp eye a type that permitted the weaving of a central thought about it, he would be haunted by it until he succeeded, by artistic means, in making this type a lever of ideas that expressed the life and tendencies of a certain period. Turgenev's method was not the method of logic. His was the method that visualized persons and scenes. That we had already noted in the "Diary" sketches. His novels are, hence, successions of scenes with individuals, each of whom represents a certain class. And because he is a great artist, Turgenev does not create a mere mechanism of abstractions but a world of human beings whose feelings, thoughts, and deeds are of intrinsic interest. His personages are so natural, their circumstances are set forth so sympathetically that even his weaklings gain a place in our hearts.

Turgenev's chief novels cover a period of about thirty years, from 1848 to 1876. They show us various aspects of the intellectual life and of the democratic tendencies during that period. *Dimitri Rudin, A Nobleman's Nest, On the Eve, Fathers and Children* were written and published before the Peasant Reforms, whereas *Smoke* and *Virgin Soil* came later. The first three are closely related in thought and form a sort of trilogy. We shall therefore find it convenient to consider them in one chapter. They show in concentrated form Turgenev's attitude toward the best representatives of advanced thought during a critical period in Russia's development.

RUDIN

When Russia's best men were condemned to inactivity and had to confine themselves to words, the type of "The Superfluous Man" grew up in great profusion. A fact of this kind could not pass unnoticed by Turgenev. Goncharov took up the study of the same type in his epoch-making novel *Oblomov* which appeared in the same decade as Turgenev's first three novels. Under conditions that prevailed in the reign of Nicholas I, a man of the "intelligentsia" mold could not possibly apply his energy, unless he entered the service of the autocratic or slave-owning state. In *Rudin* the hero who speaks so beautifully about fighting against all possible obstacles breaks

[1] *Sochineniya,* Vol. II, Preface to his novels, p. 16.

down before the first obstacle that appears in his way. Words and
no actions were indeed the characteristics of these men who were
supposed to be the best thinking element of Russian society. It was
an age of "weak" heroes.

The sketches "Petushkov (1847) "Hamlet of the Shchigri District"
(1849), *The Diary of a Superfluous Man* (1850), all intended to
show the Weak Hero, are in a certain sense, preparations for *Rudin*
(1855). They all represent the man who wills but does not act.

Turgenev was bitter against the inactive man. He spared no venom
in describing the pitiful conditions of those who merely reason, but
do not act. They are the "useless" people in the world, he will have
us understand in his *Diary of a Superfluous Man*. He picked them
among the lower classes, as Petushkov, as well as among the higher
intellectuals, as Rudin. All their talk is "smoke" unless it results in
action, was the message he would never tire of addressing to "Young
Russia." He was exasperated by that Slav characteristic of words,
words, words. If the peasant was inactive, he had to be excused
because of the narrowness of his mental horizon, the heavy oppression
of the landowner, his futility in hoping to find a helpful attitude in
the administration of the day. The small opposition he could offer
was entirely out of proportion with the vast powers vested in the
landed gentry. What chance did he stand in an open fight? And so
Turgenev uses his utmost sympathy in describing their apathy and
mute suffering. The sympathy he arouses for them is contrasted with
the almost unbelievable abuse of power exercised by the landed proprietor.

The case is different with the intellectual. The salvation must come
from the man of thought. However, thought is insufficient unless it
culminates in action, not words. The sickly figure of Chulkaturin
may symbolically stand for the sickly condition of Russian society
with its inertness. The idea touched on, in "Hamlet of the Shchigri
District," and *The Diary of a Superfluous Man,* is given artistic expression in *Rudin*.

In 1852, Turgenev wrote to Mme. Viardot[2] about his intention to
work upon a novel. But only in June 1855 he actually sat down to

[2] Letter of Mar. 17, 1852. (Halperine-Kaminsky Collection.)

it, thus thinking about the subject for some three years. Toward the end of July, the first draft was complete. It appeared in *Sovremyennik* in 1856. The book has for its setting, the period of extreme absolutism of Nicholas I, when every free word, every thought was crushed. A mere handful of men forming the intelligentsia might be said to represent the entire progressive Russia. These men felt helpless. Their thoughts and ambitions were burning lava seeking an outlet.

The scene of the story is laid in one of the estates in middle Russia, in the family of Mme. Lasunsky, a lady who takes a superficial interest in all sorts of novelties, reads books that are prohibited by censorship, and must always have around her in her "salon" all sorts of men of mark. It is in her drawing room that Rudin makes his first appearance. In a few moments he becomes master of the conversation. Everybody is dazzled by his rhetoric and the mistress of the house encourages him to talk, for these fine phrases and sentiments are really a relief from the boredom of country life.

According to Rudin, the discoveries of genius are great because they become the property of all men. The effort to discover general principles in partial phenomena is one of the radical properties of the human mind and the whole of our civilization. What people need above all is faith, says Rudin:

All these attacks upon systems are particularly vexatious, because together with the systems, people reject knowledge in general, science and faith therein, consequently, also, faith in themselves, in their powers. But people need that faith; they cannot live on impressions alone; it is a sin for them to fear thought and not to believe it. Scepticism has always been distinguished by sterility and impotence.[3]

The very progress of a nation will depend upon the faith of the citizens in themselves:

If a man has no strong principle in which he believes, no ground whereon he stands firmly, how can he understand the details, the significance, the future of his nation? How can he know what he ought to do himself?[4]

---

[3] *Sochineniya*, II, 369; Hapgood trans. III, 47.
[4] *Ibid.*, II, 370: Hapgood trans., III, 48.

Critics have found points of resemblance between Rudin and the personality of Michael Bakunin. No doubt that many of the opinions that run through Rudin's discussions deal with the very topics Turgenev must have discussed with this social leader. By his convincing remarks Rudin wins the admiration of the hostess and the sympathy of the younger generation. The latter is represented by the daughter, Natalya, and by a young student Basistov who is a tutor of the two boys in the family. Both are captivated by Rudin. And who would not be with such fascinating topics in the air as personality, welfare, sacrifice? Is there room for self-love? Yes.

Man without self-love is a cipher. At the same time, only *he* deserves the appellation of man who understands how to control his self-love as a rider controls his horse, who sacrifices his personality to the general welfare.[5]

Rudin draws a distinction between selfishness and self-love.

Selfishness is suicide. The selfish man withers up like an isolated sterile tree; but self-love, in its quality of an effective effort toward perfection, is the origin of everything great.[6]

Turgenev gives us in a few lines a remarkable description of an orator's power over his audience:

Rudin did not seek his words. They came obediently and freely of their own accord to his lips, and every word seemed to pour forth straight from his soul, glowing with all the fire of conviction. Rudin possessed what is almost the highest mystery—the music of eloquence. He understood how, by thrumming upon one of the heart's chords, to make it emit a troubled sound and set all the others to quivering. Any given hearer might not be able to understand precisely what the speech was about; but his breast heaved high, some curtains or other parted before his eyes, something radiant blazed up in front of him.[7]

When later in the evening Rudin speaks of his student years and touches upon such subjects as liberty, free thought, and the struggles in Western Europe for freedom, his words are full of so much fire, so much poetry and enthusiasm that the two younger people listen to him with a feeling which approaches worship.

[5] *Ibid.,* IV, 374; Hapgood trans., III, 54.
[6] *Ibid.,* IV, 374; Hapgood trans., III, 55.
[7] *Ibid.,* IV, 376; Hapgood trans., III, 58.

Natalya falls in love. But disappointment is in store for her. She is of the active type and will not limit herself to words. When after the first fiery speeches about poetry, life, and convictions Rudin says that it is time for him to rest, Natalya is surprised: "As to resting, others may, but you—you ought to work and try to be useful. who, else, if not you?"[8] She is ready to follow him anywhere, without making any conditions. Rudin's love is more in his brain than in his heart for he can only talk to her about the impossibility of obtaining permission of her mother for this marriage. Natalya hardly listens to his words. She will follow him with or without the consent of her mother. But at the first obstacle, Rudin throws up his hands and upon the question: "What are we to do?" he answers: "Of course to submit to fate; Natalya's bitter reproach is: "And is this how you apply your theories, about freedom, sacrifice?" To Natalya words mean actions; for her there are no obstacles. She is not afraid of sacrifices and does not hurry to submit.

Perhaps Turgenev was chastising himself in exposing Rudin's limitations. Rudin is not unaware of his weakness: "Yes, I must act," says he. "I must not hide my talent, if I possess it; I must not waste any powers in empty chatter, useless chatter, in mere words—"[9]

But he cannot bring himself to act nevertheless! That is about what the intelligentsia of the day amounted to. They were young men full of aspiration, with an impressive zeal in their search for truth. But so absorbed did they become in their idealism that they lost sight of the material aspect of life. They lived in a world of dreams and abstract speculations, becoming eventually unable to adapt themselves to life's demands. Their energies were spent in discussing *what* to do, instead of *doing*. It was an endless stream of verbiage, nothing but hamletizing.

Though Turgenev treats his hero with sympathy, he is unsparing in chastising him for his inactivity. In his reproaches we hear the admonition to the striving Russian youth: "Wake up and act!"

Turgenev feels that men like Rudin, however great be their weakness, are nevertheless needed in our march toward progress. They set

[8] *Ibid.,* IV, 392; Hapgood trans., III, 80.
[9] Hapgood trans., III, 80; *Sochineniya,* IV, 392.

an ideal before mankind. If they themselves are not of the active sort, their ideas will become productive seed as time goes on. There is no doubt that his Rudin had an influence which has blossomed into acts. Turgenev's estimate of men like Rudin is put into Lezhnev's mouth.

Genius very likely he has, but as for character—That's just his misfortune: There's no force of character in him.—But I want to speak of what is good, of what is rare in him. He has enthusiasm, which is the most precious quality in our times. We have all become insufferably reasonable, indifferent, and slothful; we are asleep and cold, and thanks to anyone who will wake up and warm us! It is high time.—He never does anything himself precisely, he has no vital force, no blood; but who has the right to say that he has not been of use, that his words have not scattered good seeds in young hearts to whom nature has not denied, as she has to him, power for action, and the faculty for carrying out their own ideas? I also maintained, I recollect, that Rudin's words could not produce an effect on men; but I was speaking then of men like myself, at my present age, of men who have already lived and been broken by life. One false note in a man's eloquence, and the whole harmony is spoiled for us; but a young man's ear, happily, is not so over-fine, not so trained. If the substance of what he hears seems true to him, what does he care about the intonation? The intonation he will supply for himself!

"That is justly spoken!" cried Basistov. "And as regards Rudin's influence, I swear to you, that man not only knows how to move you, he lifts you up, he does not let you stand still, he stirs you to the depths and sets you on fire!"[10]

Rudin typifies the failure of the Russian intelligentsia of the forties who did little more than talk.

A NOBLEMAN'S NEST

Were Russia to have no other types but those of the Rudin sort, democratic progress would have been impossible. Men had to appear who could offer qualities that would counterbalance his weakness. Such a character we shall find later in Insarov. Before offering us this hero, Turgenev wrote *Dvoryanskoe gnezdo* ("A Nobleman's Nest") in which we have the transitional type Lavretsky, who is no

[10] Garnett trans., I, 192-93; *Sochineniya*, IV, 469.

longer satisfied with mere preaching. He tried his hand in practical fields but somehow could not succeed in the currents of life into which he was thrown. Rudin's power of action was paralyzed by excess of analysis. Lavretsky had the will which Rudin lacked but was hampered by his mediocre surroundings. Nevertheless, as we shall see, he went a step further toward "the common people." In a certain sense, therefore, *A Nobleman's Nest* may be considered a sequel to *Rudin*. In the latter book we are transported into a world consisting of circles of lonely student enthusiasts spending their best energies in sultry attics, dreaming their dreams of bettering humanity. These students had absorbed Western culture and ideals and were to be the seed-bearers of Westernization in their home land. Their seeds could not spread very far, however, as the only class that offered fertile ground was the small class of the intelligentsia and solitary individuals here and there, belonging to the nobility.

In *Dvoryanskoe gnezdo* Turgenev has shown us a section of the nobility which expresses the happy side of the old system. We are in the house of Maria Dmitriyevna Kalitine, a rich widow living in a Russian provincial town. She has a beautiful daughter Liza, educated according to the standards prevalent in that day. Liza is deeply religious, representing a type whose life is largely that of the spirit. That type, because of its continuous passive existence, became incapable of any active, constructive life. It is the type who can sacrifice and suffer. Such we find Liza to be. She is one of the many passive characters that Turgenev frequently gave us in his novels and his short stories. The despotism of centuries had caused a continual repression of impulses, resulting in characters of that stamp.

There is more than a mere masterly description of a female character in the creation of Liza. There is social significance back of her individuality. Pure in her morals, devoted, free from any frivolous notions, not devoid of common sense, she possesses an enormous strength of passive endurance. So strongly have custom and tradition laid their imprint upon her individuality, that she would recoil at the mere suggestion of passing the barriers prescribed for her. Such is, we are to understand, the doom of a person who lives in a world of continual check and suppression. We dare not even take happiness when offered to us. The step must not be in contradiction with the traditional System of Approval and Disapproval. In such a system the noble individual generally conceives of duty in the form of self-sacrifice. It becomes a philosophy of self-effacement. Yet these are the women whose latent strength needs only to get the proper impetus. Theirs is a reserve strength that a country can draw upon in time of need.

Liza is wooed by Vladimir Nikolayevich Panshin, a young man with charming manners and an easy flow of egotistical talk. He brings Western notions into the house, the cheap side of Westernism. He is an unprincipled man hiding behind a veneer of culture his essentially beastly nature and, therefore, represents the Europeanized Russian in the worse sense of the word.

Presently appears Fedor Ivanovich Lavretsky, a distant cousin of Maria Dmitriyevna, who is known to live unhappily with his wife. Between his father, a despotic, narrow-minded egotist and his aunt Glafira, a harsh, fierce old woman, Lavretsky's bringing up has been a strange and solitary one; and at the age of twenty-three, he naturally fell in love with the first pretty girl he saw—Varvara Pavlovna Korobina—whom he married. As she detested Russia, they finally settled in Paris, where she became a sort of second-rate lioness. Upon the discovery of her faithlessness, he left her. Maria Dmitriyevna received him cordially and he began to frequent the house. Little by little he and Liza became enamoured of each other. One day a Parisian newspaper falls into his hands. He finds there an announcement of his wife's death. He will now be free to marry Liza. But this is all a mistake, for the lady reappears bringing with her the abominable atmosphere of the Parisian boulevard. The very soul of the woman is rouged. Lavretsky refuses to live with his wife, but Liza is lost to him forever. She enters a convent.

In a subtle manner Turgenev hints at the peasant influences upon both Lavretsky and Liza. He makes each "one of the people." He endows them with democratic sentiments for the lowly in Russia. It is for them, apparently, that the future reserved the "Kingdom of Heaven."

We said above that *A Nobleman's Nest* is in a certain sense a sequel to *Rudin*. It is one step toward action, whereas *Rudin* typifies little or no action. Lavretsky and Rudin are two contrasting characters, although similar in some respects. They are both men of high culture; both are great enthusiasts; they are not fickle but steady and persevering. The difference lies in the fact that past culture and life abroad have resulted in different consequences for each. Rudin is more of a cosmopolitan, Lavretsky more of a Russian and one of the people. Liza who is thoroughly Russian in her mental make-up feels more kinship of spirit with regard to Lavretsky than she could to a Rudin, for Lavretsky is more representative of the true Russian than Rudin. Lavretsky would identify himself with the Slavophiles, while, Rudin would align himself with the Westerners.

Lavretsky, such as we have characterized him, really embodies a great movement whose growth Turgenev was watching most jealously. The torch bearers of this movement were the Slavophiles. It was a movement toward a widening out of democratic ideas in his native land. These Slavophiles stood for Russian nationalization in its broadest phase. They resisted the intrusion of Western ideals in which they saw selfishness and moral debasement. The regeneration of Russia, according to them was to come from within and not from without. The Slavonic race was to bring a new light to the world, whereas the West would decay. Enlightening notions of the good and the true, of aspirations that were lofty and genuine, were not to be looked for in Western civilization but in the humble cottage where the unlettered peasant had not yet been corrupted by the influx of the Westernizing influence. The Slavophiles found few words of praise for Peter the Great for introducing Western customs into Russia, for these only acted as stumbling blocks to Russia's free development. They meant comfort of a different kind, necessitating the outlay of capital and, therefore, acting as an incentive to grind down the peasant.

Another important corollary of Slavophile tenets was that democracy was to come from below and travel upwards instead of coming from above and travel downwards. And so the Slavophiles were the first to spread the cry: "Go among the People." Many of them actually spent years among the peasants, with a view of studying their conceptions and their habits of life. If we keep this fact in mind, we shall be able to understand far better Lavretsky's character and actions. Though he announces that he came to Russia to cultivate the land, we are to give to the statement a much deeper significance. What Lavretsky was mainly interested in, was the cultivation of the people and not the land—to live among them, to be one of them. He is the type of reformer who, modest in his strivings, is persistent in his belief that success is to be achieved not by words but by deeds. Though these deeds may be small, yet when carried out with a spirit of sincerity and faith, they will not fail in their results. This is Lavretsky's creed. Some critics saw in Lavretsky a revolutionist, but that would hardly be the case. He is rather the representative of the class that starts the wheel of Revolution, to be set into swifter motion by his followers. Those followers we shall see in *On the Eve* (1859) and in *Virgin Soil* (1876), that was written about two decades later. What Lavretsky does among the peasants, Solomin does among factory hands.

Was Turgenev a Slavophile? Analysis of his works, his life, and his correspondence would point to the contrary. However, he was sufficiently broad in his outlook to admit the value the Slavophile movement had in Russia's further progress. It was a movement of the sentiment rather than that of the intellect. It served to shake the apathy off the Rudins who were but intellects and words. Its effects, to be sure, were not and could not be far-reaching, but it was none the less a necessary transition step. It acted as a great psychological force and had an invigorating influence upon men of progressive inclinations, who were thus given an aim and a useful outlet for their strivings. The Rudin stage had become too strong an impediment and chained men's hands and feet: its cult was the Abstract Idea. Here was a living philosophy infusing life and giving body to these spiritual notions. It pointed to an attachment for the masses, to work with the people for the benefit of the lower strata. The Slavophile movement thus raised many enthusiasts from the state of uselessness to a state of usefulness, and transferred them from a world of words to a world of deeds. Without this active influence no democracy can develop.

A Nobleman's Nest has aptly been called by one of Turgenev's critics "the poem of the youth of the Russian democracy."[11] As we

[11] Stepniak, Preface to Garnett trans. of *A Nobleman's Nest*.

turn over the pages of the novel we find Turgenev's own views and sentiments. That was part of his technique. We are particularly interested in the expression of those ideas that give us an insight into Turgenev's attitude toward the society of the day. One of his painful sores, we saw, was his witnessing the empty enthusiasm that vents itself in rhetoric. Although he gave ample expression to his hatred for this sort of "enthusiasm of words" in *Rudin* the pain is still alive while he is writing his next novel, *A Nobleman's Nest.*

In one of the episodes of the novel, Lavretsky, on coming home, is greeted by his former schoolmate Mikhalevich, who is a worthy example of the mawkishly sentimental inefficient youth of the day. A feeling of indignation is aroused in Lavretsky as he listens to the Moscow student's effusions about ideals. He is irritated by his friend's ever ready enthusiasm, perpetually at a boiling point. A typical argument about abstractions breaks out between them.

One of these endless arguments of which only Russians are capable,— with no clear understanding of the other's ideas or even of their own, catching at words and replying only in words, they disputed about the most abstract subjects, and they disputed as though it were a matter of life and death for both.[12]

The purpose of the conversation between the two friends is apparently to provide the author with an outlet for his teachings.

Has one a right to pursue personal happiness without reference to the general weal? Lavretsky had no right to do that!

MIKHALEVICH: You are an egoist, that's what it is! You wanted personal happiness, you wanted enjoyment in life, you wanted to love only for yourself! . . . And it was bound to crumble away. Either you sought support where it could not be found or you built your house on shifting sands . . . or you had no faith, no warmth of heart.[13]

To the Russian reader this is not merely a talk between two characters: it is Turgenev's voice speaking to the people.

The following is an appeal to act, addressed to the intellectual idler:

[12] Garnett trans., II, 144; *Sochineniya,* III, 293.
[13] Garnett trans., II, 145; *Sochineniya,* III, 294.

MIKHALEVICH: I have found out now what to call you. You are a loafer, and you are a vicious loafer, a conscious loafer, not a simple loafer. Simple loafers lie on a stove and do nothing because they don't know how to do anything; they don't think about anything either, but you are a man of ideas, and yet you lie on the stove; you could do something and yet you do nothing; you lie idle with a full stomach and look down from above and say:
"It's best to lie idle like this, because whatever people do, is all rubbish, leading to nothing."[14]

And so he goes on in the same strain pointing out that the intellectual youth of the day are nothing but cultivated loafers, justifying their own weakness by the fact that the same weakness exists elsewhere.

You know which leg the German limps on, and you know what's amiss with the English and French and your pitiful culture goes to make it worse: your shameful idleness, your abominable inactivity is justified by it. There are true gentlemen among us who reduce their whole life to a kind of stupor or boredom, get used to it, live in it, like a mushroom in white sauce. And this stupor of boredom is the ruin of Russians. Our age is the age for work![15]

In Mikhalevich's final crescendo, we hear Turgenev give vent to his despair at the inactivity of the Russian people, a fact he never grew tired of complaining about.

MIKHALEVICH: And what a time, what a place for men to think of loafing! . . . among us! now! in Russia! where every separate individual has a duty resting upon him, a solemn responsibility to God, to the people, to himself! We are sleeping and the time is slipping away; we are sleeping.[16]

With all that, an ironic note is clearly perceptible in Turgenev's treatment of Mikhalevich's character. For Mikhalevich himself is a beautiful example of the idle youth he is so much berating.

It is interesting to compare Lavretsky with Panshin. They represent two opposing camps. Both wish for the uplifting of Russia but look to different sources of inspiration, Panshin to the West, Lavretsky to his native land. Russia, argues Panshin, has fallen behind

[14] *Loc. cit.*   [15] *Sochineniya*, III, 295.
[16] *Ibid.*, III, 296.

Europe; it must catch up. The only justification it may offer is the fact that it is still young. But the attempt to justify it on that ground is absurd, he thinks. Furthermore, the Russians have no creative turn of mind, not even to the extent of inventing mouse traps. Hence, he concluded, they have to borrow from others and adopt European institutions. All peoples are essentially alike; all there is to be done is to introduce good models for them to follow. Panshin is the climber. He cannot stomach a philosophy that means slow evolution. Slavophilism may be productive of good in the end; but the West has models to offer now. So why wait?

Lavretsky, on the other hand, champions Russia's being independent of foreign models. Sudden leaps and reforms from above he finds impracticable, for they are founded neither on knowledge of the mother country nor on any genuine faith in any ideal. Before all, we need a recognition of the true spirit of the people and to adopt new institutions to conform with this spirit. In Lavretsky we find, as it were, a synthetic picture of all the elements that composed Russian society. Perhaps the author meant thereby to suggest that he was the outcome of a great historic process.

Upon first glance it would appear as if *Rudin* is a book of despair, and *A Nobleman's Nest* a book of renunciation. Nevertheless, there is a tone of optimism toward the end, when the aging Lavretsky greets the budding life of the new generation that will realize some of the dreams he entertained.

ON THE EVE

In June 1859, Turgenev began to write his *Nakanunye* ("On the Eve"), which he completed in December of the same year. In 1860 it appeared in the *Russkiy Vyestnik,* ("Russian Messenger").

In this novel he seeks to show the contrast between the dilettante trifling or learned pedantry of young Russia, and the intense vitality of conviction in the youth of other nations. He first introduces two young Russians, Andrey Bersenyev, a student of history, and Paul Shubin, a gay and pleasure-loving artist, who has been modeling a bust of a beautiful girl, Elena Stakhova, whose charms he dwells upon. She is the daughter of a dissipated noble; and her mother, a faded society belle, has left her to the care of a sentimental governess.

The ardent girl, filled with high aspirations, rebels at the prosaic routine of her life, and longs for intercourse with nobler natures. Both young men are in love with her. But neither is the hero of the story. The real hero is Dmitri Insarov.

Dmitri Insarov is a young Bulgarian patriot whose life is devoted to freeing his country from the yoke of Turkey. His mother has fallen a victim to the brutality of a Turkish aga, while his father was shot in trying to avenge her; and he is now looked upon by his compatriots as their destined leader in the approaching revolt. His tragic story and high aims appeal to Elena's idealism; but Insarov, finding that "on the eve" of the great conflict he is distracted from his mission by love for Elena, has resolved to leave her forever without a farewell. She, however, seeks him out and avows her devotion to him and her willingness to abandon home and country for his sake. He discovers in her the force which, far from standing in his way, would double his own energy. They will now work together for one common goal, the liberation of an oppressed race.

Their happiness is short-lived, for Insarov falls dangerously ill. His comrade and former rival Bersenyev nurses him with disinterested friendship until he is partially restored to health, when Insarov and Elena are married secretly, owing to the opposition of the family to the foreign adventurer. They start together for Bulgaria, to take part in the struggle for his fatherland, but have only reached Venice when Insarov dies. Elena, in a heart-broken letter, bids her parents a last farewell before joining the Sisters of Mercy in the Bulgarian army, as she has now no country but his. Thus ends the life story of the noblest and most ideal pair of lovers the great Russian novelist has ever drawn.

The novel has depth of meaning and gives a penetrating analysis of Russia in the fifties. As such it leaves an undying historic picture, a revelation of the secrets of the fatherland. Turgenev becomes a psychologist of his nation in bringing to the fore its highest aspirations—the desire for freedom.

Although Insarov, the fighter for liberty, is the hero of the story, one feels right along that the central figure is Elena. In her we have a fully developed type of what was only suggested in Natalya[17] and

[17] *Rudin.*

Liza.[18] Natalya has in her heart and mind the germs of what moves human beings to higher action. Rudin's spirited words, his appeals to what is grand and worth living for, inflamed her. Liza's religious bringing up and the spirit of renunciation that fills her soul make her a passive being. It is Elena who with her readiness to do deeds balances the hamletism and apathy of the weak and crushed will of the man representing the "leaders" of oppressed Russia. She is the forerunner of Marianna in *Virgin Soil:* Natalya, Liza, Elena are all women of the self-sacrificing type, women who can act in accordance with the ideals they believe in. Their will is unshaken and they are not of the continually wavering sort. In portraying these three heroines Turgenev raised a pedestal to the Russian young woman. She is higher, better, more determined, more self-sacrificing than his "weak" hero.

Elena is not satisfied with the dull trifling life in her own family and she longs for a wider sphere of action. She wants to know life in its broader phases. The portals of knowledge must be opened to her as well as to man. Woman should be free to follow her ideals on an equal footing with man. In fact, everybody should enjoy freedom, provided his acts do not interfere with the freedom of others: "You are always boasting of being a free artist; why do you encroach on the freedom of others"[19] says she to Shubin.

Book knowledge alone does not satisfy Elena. It is the use one makes of one's knowledge that counts. One must act!

Reading alone did not satisfy the girl; from childhood she thirsted for action, for active well-doing: the poor, the hungry, and the sick absorbed her thoughts, tormented her and made her heart heavy. All ill-used creatures, starved dogs, cats condemned to death, sparrows fallen out of nests, even insects and reptiles found a champion and protector in Elena; she fed them herself and felt no repugnance for them.[20]

Not of the Hamlet sort was Elena. "Being good—isn't much; doing good—yes; that's the great thing in life," she says in her diary.[21] The men she meets before Insarov do not open up to her

---

[18] *Nobleman's Nest.*   [19] *Sochineniya,* II, 261.

[20] Garnett, II, 45; *Sochineniya,* II, 270.

[21] Garnett, III, 45; *Sochineniya,* II, 270.

any fields for action. Shubin is too flighty; Bersenyev, though an excellent man, wants inspiration and lacks vigor and initiative. Both are noble and love Elena with a love that wants primarily the happiness of the other person, with a love which is not enjoyment but one which means self-sacrifice. And yet Bersenyev, though ready to sacrifice his very life for a noble ideal is not the kind who can stir others to action. He is not the sort of individual who can furnish Elena with an outlet to act and do great things.

Only when Insarov comes along, she finally meets the man who will supply her a sphere of action. All her capacity for pity that she centered before upon animals she will now direct toward suffering humanity. First now we see her in all her greatness of spirit. In Elena, as Kropotkin aptly suggests,[22] we have the true type of that Russian woman who a few years later joined heart and soul in all movements for Russian freedom: the woman who conquered her right to knowledge, totally reformed the education of children, fought for the liberation of the toiling masses, endured endless sufferings in the snows and jails of Siberia, died, if necessary, on the scaffold, and up to very recently continued with unabated energy the same struggle.

This is why the Bulgarian Insarov appeals to her. With him it is not merely words. The incident with the importunate German, Insarov's throwing the colossus into the water, merely show him as a man who expressed an idea in action instead of in rhetoric. He is the man who can fashion Elena's dreams into reality. He is not the man to waste his energies in sentimental effusions, as Shubin. Insarov is capable of a sustained purpose until its accomplishment is realized. His manner is quiet. No loud "How do you do's" are characteristic of his greeting. Each action has its definite aim. He is absorbed by one central idea, the liberation of his mother country. He casts away all philosophical speculation à la Bersenyev and marches straightforward toward the aim of his life—the freedom of his native land.[23]

To Elena there is nothing more solemn, nothing more noble, than liberating one's country. "To liberate one's country! It is terrible

[22] Kropotkin, *Ideals and Realities in Russian Literature,* p. 93.
[23] *Sochineniya,* II, 307; Garnett, III, 78.

even to utter those words, they are so grand!" she says.[24] Upon the Russian reader of that day such words must have had a powerful effect.

Insarov's strength lies in the very fact that he is on practical ground and does not soar to unattainable speculative heights. His power is by no means due to any outstanding qualities of mind. No particular talent has he, but an infinite capacity for work. "Dry as dust," says Shubin "but he can crush us all to powder. He is devoted to his country—not like our empty patriots who fawn on the people."[25] This is a sad reflection on the spiritual life of Russia and on the political conditions of the day.

In a democratic community a man of action is not master of his time. Neither is Insarov. But he will find time and walk fifty miles to settle a money dispute among his compatriots.

"And you traveled over fifty miles for such trifling matters? Wasted three days?" wonders Elena.

"They are not trifling matters, when my countrymen are involved," says Insarov. "It would be wicked to refuse in such cases. I see here that you don't refuse help even to puppies, and I think well of you for it. As for the time I have lost, that's no great harm; I will make it up later. Our time does not belong to us."

"To whom does it belong then?"

"Why, to all who need us."[26]

Insarov had good personal reasons for seeking revenge that might be considered sufficiently strong to induce him to go to his country. But he did not care to look for his personal enemy, because he felt that he had no right to think of a private wrong when a matter of far greater moment was involved—the question of avenging wrongs done to his race, or rather of freeing his race.

. . . now is not the time for private revenge, when we are concerned with the general national vengeance, when we are concerned with the liberation of a people. The one would be a hindrance to the other.[27]

His conception of one's love for country is of the broadest.

---

[24] *Sochineniya*, II, 293. [25] Garnett, III, 96.
[26] *Sochineniya*, II, 307. [27] Garnett, III, 109; *Sochineniya*, II, 309.

"You love your country very dearly?" Elena asked timidly.

"That remains to be shown," he answered. "When one of us dies for her, then one can say one loved his country.[28] What else can one love on earth? What is it one must believe in? And when that country needs. . . . Think! the poorest peasant, the poorest beggar in Bulgaria and I, have the same desire. All of us have one aim. You can understand what strength, what confidence that gives!"[29]

Insarov is not the man to be false to his cause and his duty for the sake of personal feeling. Love of country is to him synonymous with loving the oppressed and the suffering.

"I am sure you will love us, you love all the oppressed," he tells Elena. "If you knew what a land of plenty ours is! And, meanwhile, it has been downtrodden, it has been ravaged; we have been robbed of everything, our churches, our law, our lands; the unclean Turks drive us like cattle, butcher us."

To the Russian reader all these suggestions had a deep meaning. Whatever is said by Insarov could very easily apply to the oppressed in Russia. Insarov was chosen a Bulgarian, perhaps with intention, to show Turgenev's lack of confidence in a Russian man of action. That this was a sore spot with Turgenev we had already occasion to see in the analysis of his previous works. In offering this view, we feel at variance with Dobrolyubov, who sees no implication of any reproach to the young generation of Russia.[30] Perhaps he was chosen a Bulgarian in the desire to lead the censors astray. Whatever be the case, Bulgaria's wrongs were really the wrongs of Russia. Laying bare the evils of his own country at a time when absolutism was regnant with vigor would hardly be a wise policy, if his work was to see the light of day.

By making the hero a Bulgarian, in a novel that is nationalistic in its background, Turgenev achieved another bold stroke in technique—a sharp bit of irony. By throwing a foreigner upon Russian soil, Turgenev plainly indicated Russia's national weakness, at least the weakness of young Russia. We have already seen, and will con-

[28] Garnett, III, 109; *op. cit.,* II, 309.
[29] Garnett, III, 111; *op. cit.,* II, 310.
[30] *Sochineniya, N. A. Dobrolyubova,* III, 278.

tinue to see this desire on the part of our author to bring this weakness before the public. One reads in it a reproach to the intellectual youth for its inactivity; one hears a voice crying out to them to muster up their strength against a common foe and to overcome their torpor. This torpor is symbolized in Uvar Ivanovich Stakhov, who always sleeps:

"There you are lying now," cries Shubin, "in that pose; one doesn't know which is uppermost in it, sloth or strength!"

"We have no one yet, no men, look where you will. Everywhere . . . either small fry, nibblers, Hamlets on a small scale, self-absorbed, or darkness and subterranean chaos, or idle babblers and wooden sticks, or else, they study themselves to the most shameful detail, and are forever feeling the pulse of every sensation and reporting to themselves: 'That's what I feel, that's what I think.' If we only had some sensible men among us! . . . When will men be born among us?"

"Give us time," answered Uvar Ivanovich.

The next moment he put the candle out: "I'm going to sleep; goodbye."[31] Uvar symbolizes the ever-sleepy, slothful Slav, that Turgenev tries so hard to wake into action.

It is interesting to note the attitude of the contemporary reading public toward *On the Eve*. The novel found favor with the university youth, enthusiasts for freedom: the liberal and provoking tone harmonized with their own feelings.[32] The aristocratic class became somewhat alarmed at the questions that were suggested, such as the people's rights.[33]

Dobrolyubov's criticisms of *On the Eve* in Kogda zhe pridet nastoyaschi den'? attempted to justify Turgenev's choice of a Bulgarian for his hero. Why not a Russian? Because, says Dobrolyubov, the free development of individuality could not take place on Russian soil without hindrance.[34] Life was offering such complete comfort that everything was conducive toward the development of peaceful

---

[31] *Sochineniya*, II, 395.

[32] Anenkov: *Literaturnye vospominaniya* (Quoted from Ostrovski, *Turgenev v Zapiskakh Sovremennikov.*) Leningrad, 1929, p. 191.

[33] *Ibid.*, p. 167.

[34] *Sochineniya*, *N. A. Dobrolyubov*, III, 284.

sleepy individuals.[35] As a free and well regulated country in which justice and wise laws existed, Russia had no need for Insarovs.[36] In Russia, an Insarov would be an enemy of society and one whose company every well-bred young lady would shun.[37] However, one feels that there are streaks of irony behind these remarks.

Dobrolyubov places Insarov on a high pedestal. In his love for the general weal and the ability to overlook personal grievances Insarov stands above all Russian heroes.[38] As a rule, the Russian hero coming from among the educated classes spends his time in reflections about ideals, but has no strength for practical activity.[39] He who does gather sufficient courage to act, spends his energy on trifles in Quixotic fashion.[40] The best people are capable of understanding Elena's thirst for being actively good but are unable to satisfy that thirst by their own efforts. The day is not far off, hopes Dobrolyubov, when Russian Insarovs will be made possible.[41]

From Turgenev's own words we learn that very few favorable criticisms appeared, although not one of his novels called forth so large a number of critical discussions.[42] So many were there who argued against his lack of verisimilitude that he felt compelled to take up the challenge. In his preface to Stasiulevich's edition of his works in 1879, he therefore points out how he came to write the story. It was suggested to him by a diary of a certain Karatayev, who knew all the persons who served as prototypes for the novel. Among these was the hero, a Bulgarian, named Katranov. Hence his choice of a Bulgarian.

In our analysis of Turgenev's three novels written within the 2nd half of the decade preceding the Russian Peasant Reforms, we noted that the self-sacrificing ideal is strongly emphasized in each. The hero is the embodiment of a contemporary tendency, or of an ideal. "The main hero is the expression of our contemporary epoch," Turgenev writes in 1861 to Dostoyevsky, in referring to Bazarov.[43] But this could as well apply to any of his chief heroes in the novels we have discussed.

[35] *Ibid.*, p. 283.   [36] *Ibid.*, p. 283.   [37] *Ibid.*, p. 284.
[38] *Ibid.*, p. 288.   [39] *Ibid.*, III, 288.   [40] *Ibid.*, p. 292.
[41] *Ibid.*, p. 299.   [42] *Sochineniya*, II, Preface, p. x.
[43] Letter of November 18, 1861 (I. Nikolsky: *Turgenev i Dostoyevsky-Perepiska*).

Elena is Young Russia especially in its feminine aspect.

Insarov represents the patriot who does not merely watch his country's wrongs, philosophizing about them in cynical fashion, but one who acts. He embodies in himself the man of steel, the man whose purpose is law, the man whom personal emotions will not swerve from his prearranged course. Through the medium of this character Turgenev delicately suggests the type that Russia needs, not the sentimental dreamer or the Hamlet-sort of individual who wastes his energies in brooding.

We have seen how frequently Turgenev referred to his weak heroes whose inactivity was a chronic sore upon his soul. To these he opposed the Don Quixotes, developing his ideas in "Hamlet and Don Quixote" (1860).[44] In this lecture he attempts to prove that it is the Don Quixotes who advance the progress while the Hamlets retard it. Not the Hamlets but the Don Quixotes are the ones who set the revolution going:

Don Quixote is imbued with a devotion towards his ideal, for which he is ready to suffer all possible privations, to sacrifice his life; life itself he values only so far as it can serve for the incarnation of the ideal, for the promotion of the truth, of justice on Earth. He lives for his brothers, for opposing the forces hostile to mankind: the witches, the giants—that is, the oppressors. . . . He is fearless, patient. Humble in his heart, he is great and daring in his mind.[45]

And who is Hamlet? Analysis, first of all, and egotism, and, therefore, no faith. He feels his weakness, the opposite of the enthusiasm of Don Quixote. In Don Quixote, a poor man, almost a beggar, without means and relations, old, isolated, undertakes to redress all the evils and to protect oppressed strangers over the whole earth.—But in negation, as in fire, there is a destructive power.[46]

The basis of true democracy must be a willingness for self-sacrifice, a disregard of one's own interests, when the interests of numbers demand it. This is the lesson preached primarily in "Hamlet and Don Quixote." Furthermore, he would have us understand that Hamlet, by his excessive criticism of life becomes conscious of his own weakness; his will is sapped; he condemns himself to inactivity. "The Hamlets" find nothing, discover nothing, and leave no trace in their passage through the world but the memory of their personality.

[44] *Sochineniya.* X, 450-73.   [45] *Ibid.,* X, 453.   [46] *Ibid.,* X, 454.

CHAPTER V

FATHERS AND CHILDREN: A CHALLENGE TO CONSERVATISM

Toward the sixties there was a notable shake up in the social life of Russia. In the family, in the school, upon the estate, in various institutions there was a questioning spirit in evidence. With the death of the iron despot Nicholas I, in 1855, hope entered many hearts. The more progressive element insisted on a new evaluation of former notions. A period of destructive criticism was ushered in. The peasant question came in, to be sure, for its share in the discussion of the day. How was the land problem to be solved? Whose interests were to benefit most by the liberation of the peasant? Shall the reform be expected from above or is one to wait for a revolution and then contribute one's share toward its success?

A new type of man begins to make his appearance among the educated classes in Russia—the nihilist. "Nihilist" as Turgenev used the term had nothing in common with those who were associated with the terrorists who, in 1879-1881, took part in the struggle with the autocratic power. He is primarily a man who does not bow before any authority whatever, who does not accept a single principle on faith, in whatever respect that principle may be environed.[1]

The representative of the nihilists, in Turgenev's sense, is a young doctor Bazarov, a man who will bow to no authority, no matter how venerated, and who will accept no principle until it has been tested in the crucible of experience. He takes, as a result, a negative stand with reference to all institutions of his time, throwing overboard all the conventionalities and petty lies of ordinary society life.

While on his way to visit his old parents, he stops for a short stay of a few days at the country house of a young friend of his,

---

[1] *Sochineniya.* II, 25; Hapgood. VI, 38.

Arkady Kirsanov, whose father and uncle are typical representatives of the old generation. In bringing thus two generations under the same roof, Turgenev is able in a number of clever scenes to illustrate the conflict between "the fathers" and "the sons." This was a period when these conflicts were taking place in almost every educated family.

Arkady's father, Nicolay Petrovich, does his best to catch up with the young generation. Before, he rarely took an interest in practical matters, devoting his time to day-dreaming and to reading Schiller and Pushkin. He now tries to read the same materialistic books that are being read by his son and by Bazarov. But his past education makes it impossible for him to identify himself completely with the new realistic currents. His older brother Pavel Petrovich lives with him. Having spent his youth in society circles, he continues in his habits of a "perfect" gentleman, strictly obeying the conventional rules of "high" society. His hatred of Bazarov, the "nihilist," would be only natural.

Of course, Bazarov's views are diametrically opposed to his, for this daring young man does not believe in the established principles of Church and State and holds all conventional forms of society life in utter contempt. He says outright what he thinks of anybody and of anything. In thus acting he adopts an attitude of absolute sincerity, discarding all old prejudices. The ruling feature of his character is a common sense standard of judgments. His utterances are characterized by a certain roughness of expression, which only serves to irritate the members of the older generation, standing on form and polish. That was a true tendency of the time.

Curiously enough government circles interpreted the meaning of the novel in a favorable manner, for we find the following extract from an official report:

In all justice it must be said that the well-known writer Ivan Turgenev's *Fathers and Children* had a favorable influence on the minds of the readers. Standing in the foremost rank of contemporary Russian talents and enjoying the sympathies of the educated public, Turgenev, by branding our youngster-revolutionists with the biting term "nihilists," has shaken the teaching of materialism and its advocates. This, to be sure, was quite unexpected by the young generation who were applauding him recently. . . .

We must say that, in general, our literature has assumed a revolutionary tendency, subjecting to doubt the justification of a hitherto existing order. This tendency is even more dangerous than one might suppose, as it infects the younger generation and contributes to the increase of the present-day democrats by its misleading of so many minds. It is preparing, perhaps, for future Russia a series of events which, in the name of so-called liberty and self-government, deprive the people of their well-being.[2]

An interpretation of this type could not have been displeasing to Turgenev, since it would calm the censors. Very likely, Bazarov was drawn as a boor and unsocial creature to enhance the impression leading to such an interpretation as was cited above. This was only another of the extremely clever schemes he resorted to, in order to make it possible for his work to appear in print. To the enlightened reader the meaning of the work is hardly rendered obscure by these tactics. It is not impossible, however, that Turgenev was actuated by other motives, at least in part. He may have wished to represent the negative side of the young leaders, their unnecessary boorishness. There were other writers who felt the same way. Goncharov even goes to greater extremes in portraying Mark Volokhov,[3] the radical, almost turning him into a burlesque figure. Turgenev, who was a polished gentleman, could not be entirely indifferent to outward manners.

The chief meaning of the work lay in the struggle for supremacy of the views of two social strata, represented by the radical and by the conservative element. We must have a restandardization of values, according to Bazarov. Just like Ibsen's heroes in a later day he insists that no notion, no matter how sacred and time-honored, has the force of an axiomatic truth. We must take nothing on authority. Conservative classes were naturally opposed to such views. Bazarov discards all that is not of a utilitarian nature:

PAVEL PETROVICH: I do not understand how it is possible not to recognize principles and rules? By force of what do you act?

---

[2] Tsentrarkhiv ("Central Archive"), pp. 101-3. Report on activities of the 3d Division of the office of the *gens d'armes* of His Imperial Highness, 1862. (Quoted from L'vov-Rogachevsky, *Turgenev, Zhizn' i Tvorchestvo*, pp. 147-48).

[3] *Obryv* ("The Precipice").

BAZAROV: We act by force of that which we recognize as useful. At the present time, the most useful thing of all is rejection. . . . So we reject.
PAVEL PETROVICH: Everything?
BAZAROV: Everything.[4]

But he is not merely the Spirit of Denial. In the novel he is placed far above the aristocratic dandy, Pavel Kirsanov "whose nails one could send to the exposition."[5] He has little use for Nicolay Kirsanov's reading poetry—he would do better to learn more about farming! The romantic side of life offends him, for it destroys the equilibrium in a person's make-up. "Astonishing phenomenon these elderly romanticists! They develop their nervous system to the point of exasperation . . . and then the equilibrium is destroyed."[6] For this very reason he considers Nicolay Petrovich behind the times, one whose "song is sung."

Day before yesterday I saw him reading Pushkin. . . . Please explain to him that he ought not to do that. He isn't a boy; it's time for him to fling aside all that twaddle. The idea of being a romanticist at the present day! Give him something practical to read.[7]

In this attitude of Bazarov we see the trend of the times, in the sixties. Pisarev, the great critic of the day, is glad to note the decline of poetry.[8] If the poet cannot produce anything of utilitarian value he advises him to sew boots instead.[9] A work must have definite ideas that will enrich our mind. Pushkin ought to be shelved, as he does not fit into an era of analysis and investigation.[10]

We are told that Bazarov was fond of women and of feminine beauty, but love in the ideal romantic sense he considered as unpardonable folly. He regarded chivalrous sentiments as a sort of deformity.[11] He was too individualistic to want to submit to love for woman without a struggle, as every form of affection for another does of necessity imply a curtailment in the freedom of controlling one's

---

[4] Hapgood. VI, 85; *Sochineniya.* II, 56.
[5] Hapgood. VI, 27; *Sochineniya.* II, 19.
[6] Hapgood. VI, 28. [7] *Ibid.,* VI, 78.
[8] *Sochineniya.* III, 241: *Tsvyety nevinnago yumora* ("Flowers of Innocent Humor"). [9] *Op. cit.,* IV, 1. "Realisty."
[10] *Op. cit.,* 16. "Pushkin i Byelinsky." [11] *Sochineniya.* II, 105.

actions, at least where the object of affection is involved. We already saw how at one time Insarov[12] decided to give up Love to follow the dictates of Duty. Bazarov did not succeed, however, in getting beyond the mere outward signs of control. Inwardly he remained a prey to his affections and was perfectly "human."

The Bazarovs are the active people in a democracy where no idlers are tolerated, where there is no room for society lions, self-nominated guardians of the sacred laws of propriety. "The idea of my coddling these rural aristocrats! It's nothing but self-conceit."[13] Pavel Kirsanov justifies his aristocratic habits by reference to a sense of duty, of respect for one's individuality: "I respect the man in myself." To which Bazarov replies: "Here you are respecting yourself, and sitting with folded hands: What is the good of that for the *bien public?* You would do the same thing, even if you did not respect yourself."[14] All that the aristocrats feed on is high-sounding words and phrases: "Aristocracy, liberalism, progress, principles . . . when you come to think of it, how many foreign and useless words! The Russian man does not need them, even as gift."[15]

That the work is directed against the representatives of the nobility, one can hardly doubt. That reform is to come from below, from the people, is Turgenev's opinion, which he puts into Bazarov's mouth, as a parting word to Arkady.

Your fellow nobleman cannot go beyond a feeling of noble agitation, but all that is nonsense. . . . Our dust pains your eyes, our mud bespatters you, but you have not grown up to our stature; you involuntarily admire yourself; it is pleasant for you to scold yourself; but we find that tiresome—serve us up others! We must break others![16]

Bazarov is not a socialist or a populist. He is far from glorifying anything coming from "the people." He will go against them, when he sees them in the wrong.

PAVEL: Do you mean to say that you are marching against your people?
BAZAROV: And what if I am? The people assume that when the thunder

---

[12] See page 58 of this work.
[13] Hapgood. VI, 46; *Sochineniya.* II, 31.
[14] *Ibid.,* VI, 84; *Sochineniya.* II, 56.   [15] *Ibid.,* VI, 85; *Sochineniya.* II, 56.
[16] *Ibid.,* VI, 316; *Sochineniya.* II, 213.

rumbles it is the prophet Elijah driving across the sky in his chariot. What then? Am I bound to agree with them?[17]

Sometimes he despises the peasant, for he deserves to be despised.[18] There are occasions when he hates this peasant for whom he is to toil and moil and who will not even thank him for it.[19]

Bazarov is an individualist who accentuates his personal "I." Does he care much about people's opinions? "A genuine man ought not to worry about that."[20] Nevertheless, he is a torchbearer of democracy, championing the cause of the people. His "I" is the "I" of the people, of the lowest and the unrecognized. The law must adopt measures that do not deprive the lower strata of the full benefit of society's good. These people felt that Bazarov is one from amongst their midst. The servants became attached to him, although he jeered at them: they felt that, in spite of that, he was their brother, not a lordly master.[21] "Ask any one of your peasants, in which of us—in you or in me—he would the more readily recognize a fellow country-man. You do not even know how to talk with him," he says to Pavel.[22]

We are told at the very beginning of our acquaintance with Bazarov that he possessed a special faculty for inspiring the lower classes with confidence in him, "although he never indulged them, and treated them carelessly."[23] Interesting is Turgenev's own analysis of Bazarov:

Bazarov puts all the other personalities in the shade. He is honest, straightforward, and a democrat of the purest water. The duel with Pavel Petrovich is only introduced to show the intellectual emptiness of the elegant, noble knighthood; in fact, I even exaggerated and made it ridiculous. My conception of Bazarov is such as to make him superior to Pavel Petrovich. Nevertheless, when he calls himself nihilist, you must read "revolutionist." If the reader is not won by Bazarov, notwithstand-

---

[17] *Ibid.*, VI, 87; *Sochineniya.* II, 58.
[18] *Ibid.*, VI, 88; *Sochineniya.* II, 58.
[19] *Ibid.*, VI, 222; *Sochineniya.* II, 148.
[20] *Ibid.*, VI, 221; *Sochineniya.* II, 147.
[21] *Sochineniya.* II, 50; Hapgood. VI, 77.
[22] Hapgood. VI, 88; *Sochineniya.* II, 58.
[23] *Ibid.*, VI, 32; *Sochineniya.* II, 21.

ing his roughness, absence of heart, pitiless dryness and terseness, then the fault is with me—I have missed my aim; but to sweeten him with syrup (to use Bazarov's own language), this I did not want to do, although perhaps through that I would have won Russian Youth at once to my side.[24]

Bazarov comes from the lower strata, yet he not only claims equality with the nobles, but even asserts his superiority. His intellectual guides are the materialistic philosophers and naturalists, whereas the ideals of the previous generation were Hegel, Schelling, and Pushkin. Hence, he admits sensations, but denies principles: "In general, there are no principles, but there are sensations. Everything depends upon them. Why do I like chemistry? Why do you like apples? By virtue of sensations. Deeper than that, men will not penetrate."[25]

Naturally there was going to be a clash between the men of the sixties and the men of the forties. The new man does not recognize the refinements of an idealistic spirit. Science before art; use before beauty. "A respectable chemist is twenty times more useful than any poet," Bazarov maintains.[26] In his opinion, Raphael isn't worth a copper farthing.[27] He admires the Germans for their progress in the natural sciences and because "they are a practical race."[28] He believes only in facts. Everything must be tested as to its validity by reference to the senses and must be subject to experiment. The world is to him a workshop and man the master in it. A reëcho of this spirit is felt in Dostoyevsky's *Byesy* ("Possessed"), when we are told that Stepan Trofimovich was hooted out of the lecture hall for daring to maintain that Pushkin is above boots.[29]

This utilitarian philosophy found naturally strong opposition in the older generation of the forties who were fed up on idealism. This opposition was shown strongly in the criticism of the day. Dostoyevsky could not refrain from satirizing the radical leaders in his

[24] Letter to Mme. Viardot, Feb., 1862.
[25] Hapgood. VI, 222; *Sochineniya*. II, 149.
[26] *Ibid.*, VI, 44; *Sochineniya*. II, 29.
[27] *Ibid.*, VI, 93; *Sochineniya*. II, 62.
[28] *Ibid.*, VI, 43; *Sochineniya*. II, 28.
[29] Dostoyevsky: *Polnoe sobraniye sochinenii*. XII, 29.

"Possessed," in the person of Peter Verkhovensky. Bazarov is a student. That most of Turgenev's outstanding characters are students, is significant. For a long while, the literate element of Russia formed but a small percentage of the total population, and of those who could read and write only a small portion could lay claim to being considered cultivated.

There was very little of what one might call "home atmosphere" to set up ideals for the growing youth. Fathers who wished to have their children obtain an education somewhat similar to the Western type, had to send them to Moscow or St. Petersburg, or else depend upon foreign tutors. Young men of a varying bent of mind were thrown together at the large universities. Upon their return they became sensitive to the difference between culture and the brutal surroundings of Russia. No wonder they felt that the future of Russia depended upon them as an intellectual force. The students were filled early with the conviction that upon them fell the task of regenerating their country. They are the Rudins, the Insarovs, the Bazarovs. To them belonged the future, they believed.

If any of them, like Rudin, did not figure as actors in the drama, they, nevertheless, succeeded in firing others with enthusiasm, and so their life was not lived in vain. What characterized the intellectual class was a superabundance of youthful enthusiasm. They were not daunted by struggles against society, government, even against their fathers. These protests became chronical and culminated in complete negation of everything—the mood we find Bazarov in, a mood representative of the spirit of youth in the late fifties.

The nihilist type springs up then. Bazarov is a typical nihilist. Turgenev offers an explanation of the meaning of the term. It comes from the latin "nihil"—"nothing"; consequently the word designates a man who recognizes nothing.[30] According to him there is not a single institution of contemporary existence, either domestic or social, which does not challenge total rejection.[31] He does not believe the family has any solid foundation,[32] nor in the necessity of the legalization of marriage. "You still attribute significance to marriage;

[30] *Sochineniya.* II, 25.   [31] *Ibid.,* II, 62.   [32] *Ibid.,* II, 62.

I had not expected that from you."[33] says he to Arkady, when the latter remarks that his father ought to marry Fenichka, with whom he had been living as man and wife.

Does he believe in religion? Religion, too, has to stand the test of efficacy, if one is to find a place for it. He holds firm to his stand, even when on his death-bed. "Both thou and mother must now profit by the fact that religion is strong in you; here's your chance to put it to the proof,"[34] he remarks to the heart-broken father. Society must be reformed and must rid itself of all nonsensical notions. "Moral ailments proceed from a bad education, from all sorts of nonsense with which people's heads are stuffed—in a word, reform society, and there will be no disease."[35]

Bazarov believes in constructive measures. But before one can start the building-up process, the place must first be cleared.[36] And so, he will demolish! He and his followers are a force—of that he is convinced.[37] And if there are many millions who will not permit the minority to trample under foot their most sacred beliefs, and who will try to crush that minority, Bazarov is ready to submit to fate! Yet he reminds Pavel that ". . . we are not so few in number as you suppose: Furthermore, Moscow was burned to the ground by a penny candle."[38]

Those who count are the doers, not the talkers. Among the active "doers" he would not consider the noblemen. If reforms are to be brought about, they will not come through efforts on their part. They do not know how to go about things in a business-like manner. All they do is preach and deal out learned talk. As to the nihilists, they take a different stand.

It dawned upon us that it was not worth while to prate, and do nothing but prate about our ulcers; that led only to trivialities. We perceived that our leading men and accusers were good for nothing, that we were busying

---

[33] Hapgood. VI, 73; *Sochineniya.* II, 49.
[34] *Ibid.,* VI, 332; *Sochineniya.* II, 223.
[35] *Ibid.,* VI, 146; *Sochineniya.* II, 96.
[36] *Sochineniya.* II, 57; Hapgood. VI, 86.
[37] *Ibid.,* II, 61; Hapgood, VI, 92.
[38] *Ibid.,* II, 61; Hapgood. VI, 93.

ourselves with nonsense, talking about some sort of art, about unconscious creation, about parliamentarism and the devil knows what else, when it was a question of daily bread.[39]

Nicolay Kirsanov feels that the sons know better how to go about things than their fathers. They have less of the sluggishness of "noble" blood in their veins. "I feel that they have something which we do not possess, some superiority over us. . . . Youth? No: it is not youth alone. Does not their superiority consist in the fact, that in them there are fewer traces of the gentry régime than in us?"[40]

Pavel, too, realizes that not in the mere being "an aristocrat" lies a person's merit. Duty to others is far above that sentiment. "I am beginning to think that Bazarov was right when he reproached me with being aristocratic," says he to Nicolay. "No, my dear brother, it is time for us to cease putting on airs, and think of the world; it is time for us to lay aside all vanity. We will fulfill our duty and will receive happiness into the bargain."[41]

Fenichka may be of low birth, but she is a true aristocrat in the nobility and sincerity of her sentiments. Nicolay is advised to give legal status to his marriage with her. It dawns upon him that "There is no room for castes in the 19th century."[42]

What attitude do we find toward the peasant? All along we can note sympathetic touches and feel a caressing tone in the very humor that Turgenev sometimes resorts to. That humor makes these people so much more endearing to us. Their naïve wonder at the scientific facts they watch provokes a smile on the part of the reader.

"What dost thou want frogs for, master?" one of the little boys asked Bazarov.

"Why, for this. I'm going to split the frog open, and see what is going on inside of it; and as thou and I are exactly like frogs except that we walk on our legs, then I shall also know what is going on inside of us."

"But what dost thou want to know that for?"

"In order that I may not make mistakes, if thou shouldst fall ill and I had to cure thee."

[39] Hapgood. VI, 89; *Sochineniya*. II, 69.

[40] *Ibid.*, VI, 97; *Sochineniya*. II, 64.

[41] *Ibid.*, VI, 285; *Sochineniya*. II, 191.

[42] *Ibid.*, VI, 286; *Sochineniya*. II, 192.

"Art thou a doctor?"

"Yes."

"Dost hear, Vaska, the gentleman says that thou and I are just the same as frogs. Wonderful!"[43]

In the attitude of the progressive type of landowners one notes signs of the coming peasant-reforms.

"I try to the extent of my ability, not to get moss-grown, not to lag behind the age," says Bazarov's father to his son.

"Not without sensible sacrifice on my own part, I have put my peasants on quit-rent and have given them my lands by halves. I regarded that as my duty, common sense itself commands it in this case."[44]

Still these ideas of coming progress found their way very slowly into many houses. Few appreciated their significance: the peasants themselves hardly realized their benefit. The young Bazarov saw all that. He felt that the cultural level of the peasant had to be raised[45] before he could set the proper value on the coming reforms. So ingrown had become the peasant's habit of feeling himself subjugated that it was a question whether he would consider the new responsibilities of freedom thrown upon him more desirable than serfdom,[46] which meant subjection, indeed, but also security. The question arose, whether all that colossal brutish strength let loose, would not do more harm than good.

We see in Bazarov what must have been going on in the minds of hundreds of leaders who were ready to lay down their lives, if needs must be, for the general good, but who were tormented by misgivings, as to whether the *good* will be in a form they intended it to be. So long had the peasant-serf's mind been kept in beliefs planted there for generations, that at best it was by a very slow process that one could awaken his intellect to realize things in their true light. A complete reform must have for its program the education of the lowly, the training of the coming generation. Nicolay Kirsanov, we are told in the epilogue, was traveling among the peasant folk, making long speeches, in hope that by exhausting their listening powers through

[43] *Ibid.*, VI, 32; *Sochineniya.* II, 21.

[44] *Ibid.*, VI, 201; *Sochineniya.* II, 134.

[45] *Sochineniya.* II, 216.   [46] *Ibid.*, II, 216.

repetition of the same set of words to succeed in teaching the new Gospel to them.[47]

Fathers and Children was published in the spring of 1862 in Katkov's paper, *Russkiy Vyestnik*. The novel provoked a stormy controversy. It drew public attention to the profound investigation of ideas, the nature of which was something of a revelation. It seems that the public did not fully understand, and did not, therefore, fully appreciate this work of art. The Emancipation of the Serfs had been a recently accomplished event.[48] Many other democratic measures were expected to follow. The reactionists feared the ruin of the country. There grew up a great antipathy between the Old and Established Order and the fast-growing New Order.

To many critics[49] the book appeared as a contradiction. On the one hand, there was Turgenev who vowed to fight against serfdom; on the other hand, protesting against the very people who were going a step further. He felt that he was utterly misunderstood. In a letter to Marko Vovchok he speaks of his having been struck by hands he would have liked to shake.[50] The critics aligned themselves into two camps. Most regarded the work as a slander upon Russia's progressive youth.[51] However, the criticism cannot be considered as directed against Bazarov; it was rather against such characters as Sitnikov and Kukshina, belonging to a type of men and women who, by adopting the slogans and outward garb of the progressives, wished to pose as true representatives of the class. The most significant critic of this side of the camp was Antonovich, who in his essay, "Asmodey Nashego Vremeni" ("The Asmodeus of Our Day"), ridiculed the uncouth sides of Bazarov, in whom Turgenev was supposed to have shamefully misrepresented the young generation. This essay created somewhat of a sensation and provoked Pisarev's rejoinder in a lengthy article, "Realisty" ("The Realists") in which Bazarov was proclaimed the torch bearer of a new era that discarded outworn notions.[52]

[47] *Ibid.*, II, 234. [48] Feb. 19, 1861.

[49] Shelgunov, Antonovich, Zarin, Katkov, Dudyshkin, Samarin.

[50] A. Ostrovsky, *Turgenev v zapiskakh ego sovremennikov,* p. 191.

[51] *Russkiy Vyestnik;* Kropotkin: *Zapiski revolutsionera.*

[52] D. I. Pisarev. *Sochineniya.* Vol. IV.

Bazarov's character was apparently misunderstood. The Reaction-ist viewed him as a boor, as an unsocial type whose antisocial no-tions were intended to be an exaggeration of ideas that were begin-ning to circulate among the younger generation. It was the intention of the author, they contended, to ridicule these notions to the point of rendering them disgusting. Turgenev denied this interpretation. It was not a caricature of the younger generation, he said in a letter to a Russian lady.[53] Bazarov was his favorite child, he maintained. According to him Bazarov is meant to stand for a man of intellect. Equally strong was the reluctance of the younger generation to iden-tify themselves with Bazarov, who, they insisted, was a caricature and not a true representative of theirs. This misunderstanding of the character by both camps is partly explained by Turgenev's technique in developing the character. One does not get the feeling, while reading the early portion of the book, that the author's sympathy is with his hero.

The fact is that the uncritical mind links its sympathies readily with a hero who is an "Idealization," rather than a "Realization." Bazarov is *real*. His actions are brusque, indeed, but they would be exactly the kind one would expect of a man who is inspired with a great idea, who is seething with desire to act in the direction in which he sees Social Salvation, but who finds contradictions and ob-stacles at the very start. The very people for whom he would lay down his life unhesitatingly, refuse to understand him and to con-sider his coin as "true." There is, consequently, a deal of bitterness in Bazarov's mind against the very people for whose happiness he fights. The environment about Bazarov is of a provoking kind and he is excited to the nth degree by it.

Some critics saw in Bazarov nothing but the personification of Destructive Criticism. There is reason to believe that Turgenev's purpose was to make him stand for Science and its application to Social Organization. Bazarov is first and foremost a scientist—he who collects, dissects, and observes. These characteristics are defi-nitely alluded to in order to suggest the scientific spirit that pervades his nature. The cold logic of scientific investigation is then applied

[53] *Souvenir sur Tourguéneff,* by Isaac Pavlovsky, p. 112.

to society as he finds it. Of course, before new theories can be advanced, old hypotheses have to be discarded. So he discards, he denies: he will accept nothing on faith. No scientist can. It is the very essence of science to take nothing on faith. Superstitions, and confused notions of the past must be done away with! Sentimentalism of the Present must be held in check. So his first duty is that of the Destroying Angel. Only then can one get at the Truth. It is this attitude that explains his aversion to Art and Poetry; they appeal to sentiment and foster sentimentality. Sentimentality must not be permitted to blind the intellect. Hence, nothing of the past is sacred to him except in so far as it can find application to a new universal order of things. Customs of the past are to him ridiculous. The Law of the Past has held the mind chained in its grasp.

Only by looking upon Bazarov as the emblem of the Scientific spirit can we understand those actions of his which fail to invite our sympathy, such as his apparent harshness toward his parents. Ties of love or of family must not be permitted to hinder the advancing steps of the strong leader. There is no room for poetic sentimentality in his soul. These do not strengthen; they weaken action.

He will only succumb to the stronger Law of Nature that renders man powerless. He dies grappling with nature, but his influence has remained, and so he still lives on. Bazarov's notions can be traced in the social movement of today, in the scientific spirit of the age, in the subjection of everything to minute analysis; in beliefs of such figures as Ibsen in Norway, Hauptmann and Wassermann in Germany, Brieux in France, Shaw in England.

The man of Bazarov's stamp, like the famous Stockman in Ibsen's *Enemy of the People,* prefers to stand alone. He is not in search of honors; the laurels of public success do not lure him: public opinion is a matter of indifference to him. Even love itself must not come between him and his cause. It is only Death, the Arch Destroyer, that can and *does* cut his career short. Bazarov knows his own powers, he feels them waning—he knows that he is a Guiding Lamp to others, a lamp whose flame flickers. "Blow upon the dying lamp" he says to Odintzova," feeling that consciousness will soon leave him. He remains after his death a Guiding Lamp.

That *Fathers and Children* has Reform as its dominant keynote, there seems to be very little doubt. That theory becomes more apparent upon the analysis of Bazarov's character. Viewed in proper prospective, Bazarov appears mainly as the Reformer. All other characters are used either to place Bazarov's into stronger relief or merely to bring his notions to the front. Indeed, he stands like a giant among pigmies. Every one is made to feel his superiority. Everything is made to center about him. The older Kirsanovs face him as emblems of the past cult of Aristocracy and Traditions of Birth. Arkady represents Sentimental Youth of the Present, whose energy spends itself in admiration and emotional effusion. The Family hearth is represented in the persons of Bazarov's father and mother. All these are forces that the reformer has to reckon with. Each one has its noble tale to tell, but is a hindrance to the reformer. He stands upon a height and looks into the distance where he sees bigger things in comparison with which these play but a very insignificant rôle. He is the most dominating of Turgenev's creations.

Among the great critics of the day Pisarev was the only one who understood Bazarov as Turgenev wanted him to be understood. Pisarev analyzes Bazarov as an empiricist who recognizes only those things whose existence can be proved by his senses. Bazarov needs nobody. He is afraid of no one, he has no love for anybody, and, therefore, knows no mercy. His ironical attitude towards all sorts of emotions, towards sentimental dreams, lyrical strivings, confessions, is a manifestation of his inner cynicism. The crude expression of this irony, the unwarranted and aimless roughness of his manners mark his outward cynicism.

Many were curious to know whether Bazarov was a pure invention of Turgenev's. He used to tell to his intimate friends that he could never write to his satisfaction, unless he had a living model to work from. In 1869 he writes:[54] "I never attempted to create a type without having a living person to work from. At the foundation of the principal figure of Bazarov was the personality of a young provincial doctor, who died not long before 1860."

He met him in a railway carriage, while traveling in Germany. Turgenev entered into a conversation with him and was struck by his

[54] "Literaturnya i zhiteyskiya vospominaniya," *Sochineniya.* X, 101.

keen and original opinions. This character of Bazarov, to such extent absorbed Turgenev that he kept a sort of "Bazarov Diary." If he read a new book or met an interesting man, he would describe them from the point of view of Bazarov. Turgenev's creation of Bazarov from a short two hours' meeting with a man, while on a trip, is an interesting example showing how powerfully he could develop a system in his imagination. From this solitary meeting with an individual Turgenev predicted the progress of the most formidable social and political movement in modern Russia, and set it forth in art a number of decades before its birth.

Interesting is the comparison of the three characters, Rudin, Bazarov, and Insarov. They appear to supplement each other. Each is the concrete embodiment of an ideal—the public orator, the daring inquirer, the man of action. Society needs all these men alike. Though Rudin spends his energies in talking, his words are not lost. Here and there they fall on fertile ground. The seed takes root and the growing product carries Rudin's ideas into action. Bazarov sets the mind doubting. A revision of old notions with a consequent casting off of worn out prejudices is the result. Insarov shows the idea ripened into form. To him action is the essence of strength; and so he is a man of few words. All are types strictly individualistic. Rudin makes his opinions predominate over others, whose doctrines grow pale and worthless under his sharp scrutiny. Bazarov stands as a god to whom the followers in his circle look up. As to Insarov, there is nothing that can make him swerve from his prescribed course of action.

In every great movement there is to be found a deal of "chaff." Many there will be who enter the ranks for selfish motives of one kind or another, people whose affiliation is evidenced only by the slogans that they frequently spew out. Of this type are Avdotya Nikitishna Kukshina and Victor Sitnikov. Kukshina, upon first acquaintance, calls Bazarov by his surname, as if to imply that she did not adhere to conventions, that she was an emancipated woman. She smokes, she dabbles in chemistry, reads Liebig, pretends to be interested in the woman question, in schools, and in no end of other "liberal" tendencies.

Fathers and Children shows Turgenev in the very midst of social life, recording the political and social movements of his time, giving voice and artistic interpretation to the foremost ideas of the society he lived in. Several generations owe him a part of their intellectual inheritance, as their growth was and is, perhaps, still going on under the unchanging powerful influence of the psychic impulses which are diffused in his works. Along with the charm of intimate human feelings he taught them the value of a free personality, of liberty in the broadest sense. One is reminded, in this connection, of Rudin's words to Basistov: "Liberty is one of man's most precious possessions, and happy is he on whom heaven has bestowed a morsel of bread, who is not compelled to be indebted for it to any one!"[55] His figures embody forces in which his fatherland is poor, which the soil needs for enrichment, which the race is urged to develop. Viewed from this point of view Turgenev becomes the sympathetic Father of his country which he regards as a sick patient, for whose ills he tries to suggest remedies.

One might consider him in the double rôle of psychologist of individuals as well as of classes that compose the Russian nation. Drawing in broad lines, he cannot, therefore, center his best energies in some one character, where human nature would be studied in so far as it reveals differentiation of the species. He feels he has a mission. His chief characters are, therefore, universal characters and embrace whole classes. His method is that of creating an individual and then endowing him with qualities that make him a representative of a class, a type. Frequently he clothes the character with attributes that he should like to see universalized. He endeavors to depict this character with all the power, all the colors at his command. He arouses in the reader deep admiration for his character. He awakens a desire to act as the character acts. He appeals to our wills. Hence his greatness as a reformer. He gives his character a purpose, an aim in life. Thousands of young men and young girls have taken up this or that character and made it their model.

Not only did Turgenev show himself a great reformer but an artist of the first make. As such, he understood that straightforward discussion can appeal only to readers who are trained to a reflective

---

[55] Hapgood. III, 190; *Sochineniya*. IV, 454.

type of literature. The more effective way is to make an appeal to the emotions by means of the story form. Although the tendency of his novels is to carry a social message, the artist never loses sight of the fact that he is not there to preach. The reader is in a current of real human life with all its complications. There are very few works that can compare with Turgenev's in this respect. They scrutinize to the very bottom the economic and social conditions and reproduce with remarkable vividness the spiritual struggles of men and women in their onward march to national progress.

CHAPTER VI

TURGENEV'S IDEAS DURING THE POST-REFORM PERIOD:
SMOKE; VIRGIN SOIL; PUNIN AND BABURIN;
TALES; POEMS IN PROSE

The abolition of serfdom, February 19, 1861, gave rise to the hope
for other reforms. The years that immediately followed were, therefore, years of great intellectual unrest. A régime that held millions of
people in bondage was broken. The intellectuals now felt an urge to
do great things along social as well as economic lines. Such an intellectual we have seen in Bazarov. To be sure, along with these there
were the Hamlets, who inherited from the serf days the fatal disease
of inactivity, which they could not throw off. A revision of earlier
theories became necessary, now that they were brought face to face
with actualities. To many this caused disillusionment and many minds
became filled with sorrow, melancholy, and despair. This disenchant-
ment is seen in Turgenev as well as in the heroes of his later works.

Turgenev's pessimism is very apparent in the sixties. He was brok-
en-hearted over his being misunderstood in his *Fathers and Children.*
"I felt then very discouraged," he says in his *Literary Reminiscences.*"
I was noticing coldness, reaching the point of indignation, in many
of those with whom I stood in sympathetic relations. I was receiving
congratulations and was being embraced by people from the camp
toward which I felt antagonistic. All this threw me into confusion and
pained me."[1] He grew bitter and became more outspoken, manifest-
ing greater boldness and directness in his actions. The Russian government was not blind to that fact. In 1862 he was summoned to
St. Petersburg to explain before the senate his relations with the
émigrés Bakunin and Hertsen. Now and then there is a glimpse of
optimism. Thus in Feb. 1864 he shows a certain hopefulness, when

[1] *Sochineniya.* X, 102.

he writes to his aunt, the wife of Nicolas Turgenev: "A tout prendre, la position de la Russie s'est beaucoup améliorée et c'est ce qui est le plus important pour le patriotisme éprouvé de votre mari."[2]

To be sure he never regretted the liberation of the serfs. To him the anniversary was a holiday, he never failed to celebrate.[3] Nevertheless, he was too wide-awake and observant of the course events were assuming not to feel strongly disappointed. A pessimistic mood pervades his letters and his works. In "Phantoms,"[4] one of his "dream tales," the hero is carried from country to country. When he reaches Russia he says:

Sadness came over me and a kind of indifferent dreariness. The whole earthly globe with its population, multitudinous, feeble, crushed by want, grief and diseases, bound to a clod of pitiful dust . . . these human flies, a thousand times paltrier than flies; their dwellings glued together with filth, the pitiful traces of their tiny monotonous bustle, of their comic struggle with the unchanging and inevitable,—how revolting it all suddenly was to me! My heart turned sick, and I could not bear to gaze longer on these trivial pictures, on this vulgar show. . . . Yet, I felt dreary, worse than dreary. . . . There was in me a feeling of loathing, and stronger than all and more than all within me was the loathing for myself.[5]

Everything is enveloped in gloom. Pictures of horror haunt him: "Something bulky, dark, yellowish black, spotted like a lizard's belly, not a storm-cloud, and not smoke, was crawling with a snake-like motion over the earth.—A movement recalled the malignant sweep of the wings of a vulture seeking its prey."[6]

Cheerless is the impression we get from "Enough," written in 1864. It describes the sentimental effusions of an artist. He sees scarcely anything that is worth living for. The theme of the sketch appears to be: "What's the use of it all!—Enough of life's sufferings!" " 'Enough!' Enough of bustling and stretching,—it is time to

[2] Feb. 6, 1864 (quoted from Brodsky: *Turgenev i ego vremya*).
[3] Letter to Mlle. Fanny, Feb. 18, 1873 (Brodsky).
[4] Written in 1863. "Phantoms" Trans. of Constance Garnett. X, 152-53.
[5] *Sochineniya*. VI, 420.
[6] Garnett. X, 154; *Sochineniya*. VI, 421.

lay down and shrink into oneself; it is time to take your head into both hands and bid the heart be still."[7]

All our activity is a matter of self-delusion. We are all in the hands of fate; only, busy as we are, we do not feel its rough hand. Life is possible only to the extent to which one is able to fool oneself into a belief that he is useful. "Once the truth flashed upon us, there is only one thing left for us to do—to sink into self-contempt, to turn from everything and say: "Enough!""[8] All that is left is a person's consciousness of his own nothingness. He recalls Shakespeare's lines:

> Life's but a walking shadow, a poor player
> That struts and frets his hour upon the stage
> And then heard no more; it is a tale
> Told by an idiot, full of sound and fury,
> Signifying nothing.[9]

But are there not any noble ideas worth striving for, such as nationalism, right, liberty, humanity, art? True, but these reduce themselves to mere words and people live with these words and for the sake of these words.[10] The sketch concludes with the extremely pessimistic thought: "Only that lives in this world, which has no right to live. We do not know what we are striving for. Each one of us rushes along to an unknown goal! Enough! . . . "The rest is silence."[11]

SMOKE

Smoke was written in 1866. The action refers to 1862. All the bitterness that accumulated in Turgenev's soul was poured out at boiling temperature. He scrutinized with mocking eyes the young patriots of Russia and voiced his disillusionment in his political dream. All the high flown rhetoric of Russia's liberators seemed to him as so much smoke. He heard too much of that when watching some of the emancipated *émigré's* in Baden. All the rich hopes he heard mentioned by the young political enthusiasts, their exaggerated ambitions, their remedies for the evils, the achievements of the past, present, and those anticipated in the future—all was mere smoke to him. In his mind the Peasant Reforms were to be the beginnings of more

[7] *Sochineniya.* VI, 425.   [8] *Ibid.,* VI, 433.   [9] *Macbeth.* V, 5.
[10] *Sochineniya.* VI, 433.   [11] *Ibid.,* VI, 439.

extensive liberal reforms. But affairs did not move at a pace sufficiently rapid to suit him. Hence his disappointment, which found complete expression in *Smoke*.

In our study of previous works of Turgenev we noticed already that the plot was only a frame or binding for his ideas. In *Smoke* page after page is full of discussions on political and social topics that interest our author. It is only the great artist in Turgenev who saves the work from becoming a mere political pamphlet. He knew how to give life to his characters and how to link ingeniously what would seem isolated events.

The story in its barest outline would run somewhat thus: Litvinov, a student of twenty, falls in love with Irene Osinina. His love is reciprocated. An opportunity to enter high society presents itself. Irene's parents induce her to break with Litvinov.

Ten years later he meets her in Baden, as the young general Ratmirov's wife. She makes attempts to awaken Litvinov's former love for her. Although he had already accustomed himself to his life without Irene, had already made his choice, and is about to marry Tatyana, his old love awakens. A conflict takes place in his mind. Upon Tatyana's arrival he tells her, not without hesitation, how matters stand. Tatyana releases him from all obligations, and leaves town.

Litvinov has sacrificed everything. When he asks Irene to leave the life in the hypocritical circle in which she turns, she hasn't the courage to do so. She offers him the proposition of leaving for St. Petersburg, where she will continue in her sphere, but will see him frequently. Litvinov first now realizes that he is being used by Irene as a tool to ward off boredom. He makes a strong move, leaves town on the way to his small country place where he is going to labor and improve the land. He is thus saved from fall. On the train he sees his past as smoke that is now beginning to clear.

After three years an opportunity presents itself to see Tatyana. She is his guardian angel. With her his former self, his strong self, will once more be active for the good of all. She receives him with open arms and pardons him everything.

Very few characters in this novel have escaped the venom of the writer's spleen. He spares neither foreigner nor his own country fellowmen. With the exception of Litvinov, there is hardly a character who has not been caricatured. Bambayev is the fellow who is always busy, but doing nothing. He is a "nice" man with cheeks and nose as soft as though they had been boiled. Gubaryev is a gentleman of respectable and rather stupid appearance. This Gubaryev, by the way, is the incomparable scholar whom Bambayev worships. Turgenev's scorn of the fussy idlers that one meets everywhere is sometimes shown by the name he assigns to his characters as Madame Sukhanchikov whose eyes it was "unnecessary" to mention: they were always jumping.

Smoke excited a great deal of discussion as to whether Turgenev was a true Russian. The continual reminders of Western superiority that run through the pages of the book have led to that charge. His friendship with Dostoyevsky and other literary figures suffered because of his apparent alienation from Russia. Turgenev denied the charge. He was simply in despair at the incompetency of the Russian intelligent youth to shake off its torpor, and develop a flourishing democratic civilization on their own soil, without recourse to foreign models for imitation. In *Smoke* he hoped through irony and sarcasm to make the rising leaders feel ashamed at their lack of self-reliance. Litvinov, a promising young man, to gain experience and skill, must go abroad to study agronomy and technology, hoping then to convert his mother's badly managed property into a gold mine. And so he spends about four years in Germany, Belgium, England, laboring conscientiously to acquire information.

It was left for the younger generation to work out the problem of adaptation into a new order of things. The fathers were disconcerted by the emancipation, by the division of lands, by an economic order that made a complete abolition of former methods of management absolutely imperative. Western methods of management could teach Russia a useful lesson. And so Litvinov, having acquired the needed information, now confident of his future, and of his usefulness to his fellow-countrymen, is ready to return to his native land.

In an apparently off-hand manner Turgenev suggests the import and social question of woman's economic independence. "All women," says Mme. Sukhanchikov, "must supply themselves with sewing machines. In that way they will earn their living and become independent. Otherwise they cannot possibly free themselves."

Sometimes Turgenev likes to direct a thrust at Russia's immaturity —politically speaking. "It seems to me," says Litvinov, "that it is still too early for us Russians to have political opinions, or to imagine that we have them." Turgenev gives a picture of typical meeting of future "Saviors" of Russia with Gubaryev in their midst. There is a deal of shouting, loud-mouthed discussions about most irrelevant topics, enough to drive one mad. The future "doers" are mercilessly lashed. The student leaders, represented by Voroshilov, appear at these gatherings, apparently to aid in the solution of pressing problems of the day, but are in fact only seeking the opportunity to display the superficial knowledge they gathered, by shouting catalogues of names into the air.[12] Litvinov is glad to slip away unnoticed. "What sort of thing was it they were present at? Why did they meet together? Why did they shout and quarrel? Why did they get so excited? What's the use of it all!" Litvinov asks himself. To what may one ascribe the influence that a nonentity like Gubaryev is able to exert upon them?

The answer is put into Potugin's mouth. Gubaryev, he says, has a great deal of will, whereas the Slavs, in general, lack it. They bow before the first individual who offers a manifestation of will. And so this Gubaryev desired to be a leader, and every one has recognized him as a leader. Although the government released the Russians from serfdom, the habits of serfdom have remained too deeply rooted in their system to enable them to throw off their pernicious influence. In everything and everywhere the Russians want a master. Sometimes they become slaves to a certain tendency without knowing the why and wherefore of it. "Ours is a slave nature, apparently,"[13] Potugin concludes. One can easily see that through all this talk of Potugin's Tugenev is only chastising his own fellow countrymen.

Turgenev lets us know in this novel what his attitude toward the Slavophile is:

They are very true people, but there is the same picture of despair and irritation. They live in the future only. They never utilize the present.

---

[12] *Sochineniya.* III, 24.   [13] *Ibid.,* III, 30.

In the course of centuries they did not work out a single thing they can call their own; neither in government, nor in the courts of justice, nor in science, nor in art, nor even in the handicrafts.[14]

The cry of the Slavophiles was that reform must come from below. Turgenev did not share that view very much. Ironically Potugin says: "Do you see that peasant coat? That's what all will proceed from. Let us have faith in the peasant coat."[15] What we need, thinks Tugenev, is to become humble and adopt from our elder brothers that which they have invented better than we and earlier than we.

Turgenev anticipated objections. These are voiced by Litvinov:

LITVINOV: Here you say that we ought to borrow, to adopt from our elder brothers; but how can we adopt without taking into consideration the conditions of climate and soil, and local and national peculiarities? It is impossible to adopt things haphazardly.

Potugin undertakes to answer this objection.

POTUGIN: And who forces you to adopt haphazardly! Surely you take a foreign thing not because it is foreign but because you find it suitable: consequently you do take the circumstances into consideration, you do make a selection. And so far as the results are concerned, pray do not disturb yourself; they will be original by virtue of those very local, climatic and other conditions to which you allude.

Potugin continues his line of reasoning with respect to language importations.

POTUGIN: Just take our language as an example. Peter the Great deluged it with thousands of foreign words—Dutch, French, and German: those words expressed conceptions with which it was necessary to make the Russian nation acquainted; without philosophizing and without standing on ceremony. Peter poured those words wholesale, by the bucketful, by the cask, into our bosom. At first, it is true, the result was something monstrous, but later on the conceptions became grafted on and appropriated; the foreign forms gradually evaporated; the language found in its own bosom the wherewithal to replace them—and now, your humble servant will undertake to translate any page from Hegel without making use of a single non-Slavonic word.[16]

---

[14] *Ibid.*, III, 32.   [15] *Ibid.*, III, 32.
[16] *Ibid.*, III, 33.

That which has taken place with language, Turgenev argues, will take place in other spheres.

And now follows that portion in his book for which Turgenev was so sharply assailed, mainly his extreme leaning toward Westernization. It is again Potugin who speaks:

POTUGIN: You asked my opinion concerning Europe. I am amazed at it and devoted to its principles to the last degree, and do not consider it necessary to conceal the fact—to speak more accurately, I am devoted to culture, to that same culture at which people so charmingly jeer nowadays in our country,—to civilization. It is intelligible, and pure, and holy, but all others, whether it be nationality, or glory, smell of blood. I want nothing to do with them!

LITVINOV: But you love Russia, your native land?

POTUGIN: I love it passionately, and hate it passionately.[17]

It is this last remark of Turgenev's that was so much misunderstood and that caused a break between him and some of his Slavophile friends. In so far as we can judge from Turvenev's life and letters we can put only one interpretation on this remark: He loved Russia and shared the happiness of its people, but he hated their apathy and inactivity; he hated their inability to break through the shackles that kept their energies chained: he hated the wasting of vital forces in mere talk.

We get a glimpse of the point of view the military faction takes with regard to the peasant reforms and the spread of democratic feeling. Some regard it as a delusion that has befogged the people's minds, that a certain "blindness" has taken possession of even the loftiest minds. It becomes, therefore, necessary to take precautionary measures, and to point out to the citizens the abyss whither everything is hastening. As to the freedom that was granted to the peasant by the Emancipation Laws, it is questionable whether that freedom is sweet to the people! Universities and seminaries and schools for the common people ought to be restricted in their field of activity. As to self-government, no one asks for it anyhow! The old ways of times gone by are the best after all! They are much safer.[18] "Do not permit the common people to reason, and put your trust in the aris-

[17] *Ibid.*, III, 36. [18] *Ibid.*, III, 70.

tocracy, in which alone there is power.—Most of all do not meddle with discipline."[19]

Those reflections are uttered by a half-intoxicated young general of Ratmirov's group. Turgenev thus suggests diplomatically the attitude of the government authorities toward the people's rise to power. It was a bold stroke and yet it is put in such a form as to avert the suspicious eyes of the censors. He had recourse, more than once, to such methods in order to achieve his purpose. At the same time Turgenev loses no opportunity of hinting sarcastically at the kind of liberalism the military aristocracy practised. It did not prevent the young general Ratmirov from soundly flogging fifty peasants in a revolted White Russian village, which he had been sent to pacify. He partly lifts the veil, so we may see the life of this "high society." We are given a chance to see what useless nonsense, what insipid trifles fill all those brains, and that, not for one evening only, not only in society, but at home, at all hours, every day in all "the breadth and depth of their beings:" "What ignorance in conclusion! What lack of comprehension of everything upon which human life is founded, by which it is adorned!"[20]

Through humbleness of spirit and a willingness to acknowledge the superiority of foreign models Russia can eventually develop her own culture. The so-called national unconscious creative genius is stuff and nonsense.[21]

In Potugin's parting advice to Litvinov we hear Turgenev's prophetic voice as to the future of Russia and her growth upon European models.

POTUGIN: On every occasion, when you are obliged to enter upon an undertaking, ask yourself: are you serving civilization, in the exact and strict sense of the word, are you furthering one of its ideas; is your labor of that pedagogical *European* character, *which alone is profitable and fruitful in our day*, in our country? If so, advance boldly; you are on the right road, and your affair is an honorable one! You are not alone now. You will not be a "sower" in the desert! Hard workers . . . pioneers . . . have already sprung up among us.[22]

---

[19] *Loc. cit.*   [20] Hapgood. VII, 175; *Sochineniya*. III, 115.
[21] *Sochineniya*. III, 103; Hapgood. VII, 156.   [22] *Sochineniya*. III, 187.

With the last words Turgenev is, of course, speaking to the energetic, ambitious youth of Russia, wishing to encourage them to action for their country's weal.

In *Smoke,* one object was to represent the Russian society lioness, a type which had haunted Turgenev for years and which he finally depicted in a fuller and more perfect form in *Veshniya Vody* ("Spring Freshets"). His other object, the one we are mainly interested in, was to picture in its true colors the shallowness of that society of bureaucrats into whose hands Russia fell after the peasant reforms. Deep despair in the future of Russia, after the great reform movement which resulted in the abolition of serfdom, pervades the novel. It is due to bitter disappointment consequent upon the wreck of Turgenev's hopes in the achievements expected from the friends of the reform movement of 1859-1863. As a central problem, we have the future of Russia and the lines of its development; along with that we noted endless disputes between the Westerners and the Slavophiles. He takes sides with western Europe and advocates personal freedom, as interpreted by the West. One readily recognizes Turgenev's views in Potugin's long-winded effusions.

Turgenev entertains hopes for Russia's enlightenment, for its gradual adoption of Western ideals of culture. However, the rights of the individual must be respected: that is something Turgenev always stood for. In 1856 he writes: "I have fought for the rights of the individual and will continue to fight to the end."[23]

VIRGIN SOIL

In the seventies Turgenev was a collaborator of the liberal periodical *Vyestnik Evropy* (the "European Messenger"). The monthly magazine was a strong advocate of such ideals as liberty of conscience, freedom of speech and of the press, social adjustment, protection of labor. Turgenev was considered one of its chief contributors. His writings appeared during the most important months at the beginning and at the end of the year, when subscriptions were solicited. His interest in the periodical was very great. From 1868 on, his chief works were published there. His close relations with the periodi-

[23] Letter to S. T. Aksakov; Brodsky, *Turgenev i ego Vremya,* p. 117.

cal are proved by more than 300 letters addressed to the editor, Stasiulevich, and preserved by him.

In 1876 *Virgin Soil* was completed. It appeared in the *European Messenger* in the January and February issues of 1877. It immediately called forth a number of contradictory criticisms showing the various interpretations to which the work lent itself. However, one thing is clear, that the book was intended to reflect the epoch of the seventies. It immortalized the image of the revolutionary girl in the person of Marianna.

Nov' ("Virgin Soil") was preceded by the Franco-Prussian War. Turgenev's stand was for the Germans. His views appear in *Sankt Peterburgskie Vyedomosti*.[24] There he says: "Only in the complete fall of the Napoleonic system do I see civilization saved and a possibility of developing free institutions in Europe."[25]

After the failure of the French Commune in 1871, Switzerland became the gathering place of the emigrated Russian revolutionists. Zurich was the centre for the work preparatory to new attacks. It is to this place that student youth flocked in large numbers, particularly young women who did not succeed in getting their higher education in Europe. Among these young people political ideas spread rapidly. These ideas were fanned into enthusiasm by the Franco-Prussian War and by the French Commune. "Among the people!" became the slogan of the day. As early as 1861 Hertsen threw this slogan into circulation. Now Zurich was preparing ranks of inspired rosy and dreaming youth to go among the people, with a readiness to sacrifice home, comforts, life—if necessary. Bakunin was then the hero of the revolutionary youth. His was a mortal hatred for government in all forms. He encouraged the cry—"to the people," "to the country."

In 1871 Nechayev one of the hitherto most trusted revolutionists turned traitor to his cause betraying some of its intimate doings to the Russian government. It was this Nechayev who became the prototype of the monster Peter Verkhovensky in Dostoyevsky's *Byesy* ("The Possessed"). The administration immediately started investigations. In 1873 an order was issued for the young students to return from Switzerland. This eventually led to court proceedings in 1877,

[24] Nos. 216, 219, 231, 252, 262.   [25] No. 231, *Sankt Peterburgskie vyedomosti*.

in which sixteen Zurich girls, from the students of 1872-73, were involved.

All this stir did not escape Turgenev's attention. In 1872 he contemplated a new novel. In 1873 he intended to go to Zurich to become more closely acquainted with the students. The growth of opposition to the reigning despotism found a responsive chord in him. However, he was more on the side of the moderates. He was not much in sympathy with Bakunin, who was an extremist and who urged immediate action. He was more impressed by Lavrov, a prolific and rather peaceful propagandist. In 1874 Turgenev entered into correspondence with this Lavrov, whose work he found useful. In that year he wrote to him, commenting on his article in which propaganda versus uprisings was being discussed: "You are perfectly right. But youth will almost always find it difficult to understand that it is possible by slow and patient methods to prepare for something strong and sudden."[26]

He became a financial contributor to Lavrov's liberal periodical *Vperyed* ("Forward"), as is evidenced by the letter of February 21, 1874.

In the heat of my enthusiasm I promised you yesterday a little more than my means permit: 1000 francs I cannot give you but will contribute gladly 500 francs until your undertaking, to which I wish success, is upon a self-supporting basis. Enclosed find 500 francs for the year 1874.

We find him in correspondence with other fighters for the "people's cause." Among these was one who deserves attention, Anna Pavlovna Filosofova, who supplied Turgenev with source material used in *Virgin Soil*. This woman was an example of many who vowed to give all their strength to the people. She took an active part in spreading culture among the masses, in organizing cheap dwellings for the poor, in being instrumental in the establishment of higher educational courses for women. In 1878, the Russian government compelled her to leave St. Petersburg and go abroad, inasmuch as she was found "guilty" of displaying her sympathies toward revolutionary folk, in helping the families of those who were being sent to Siberia, in aid-

[26] Letter of Dec. 5, 1874, from Turgenev's Letters to Lavrov in *Byloe* of 1906.

ing the families of those who had been arrested, and of those who had been sentenced to death.

In 1874 Filosofova sent Turgenev a portfolio containing her diary and documents and manuscripts, with a view of acquainting our author with the personalities and ways of thinking of the "new people" whom he, living abroad, could not possibly know well. Turgenev sifted the material very carefully and took note of information to be used in connection with *Virgin Soil*. The braggart Kislyakov in the novel was a counterpart of a certain propagandist Leo, referred to in these documents. Does he still believe that men of the Bazarov type will bring about the greatest good? The time for the Bazarovs has passed. What we need now is "useful people."

Times have changed; the Bazarovs are not needed. For the coming social activities no particular talent is wanted, not even any clever minds—nothing colossal or conspicuous, no great individual attainments. What is wanted is industry and patience; one must be able to sacrifice oneself, be humble and not fear menial tasks.[27]

Turgenev did not believe in extreme and rapid action. It is the gradual, step by step, method that he now advocated. He was, therefore, strongly in favor of mass education: the dark masses must be enlightened. All these ideas, moods and observations he incorporated in *Virgin Soil*, which he began early in 1876, and regarding which 52 letters were written to the editor of the European Messenger, Mr. Stasiulevich, and others to Mr. Anenkov. The novel was completed in July, 1876. About half a year passed in making various changes to suit the opinions of the censors and in 1877 the work appeared in the January and February issues of the *European Messenger*.

Turgenev's views are developed by Solomin, who is a calm "gradualist" coming from the people. For years he has been in the midst of workmen and has studied the problems of factory life. He is the first proletarian hero in Russian literature. In him Turgenev anticipated a type that became prominent in modern Russian literature. Ivanov-Razumnik views him as a forerunner of the rising middle class.[28]

[27] Letter to Miss Filosofova, Sept. 11, 1874 (Quoted from L'vov-Rogachevsky, p. 181.)

[28] Ivanov-Razumnik: *Russkaya Literatura, ot semidesyatykh godov do nashykh dney*, pp. 210-12 (Berlin [Skify] 1923).

Turgenev, in depicting him, felt the approach of a new social stream, one in which the industrial strata would have a strong part to play. He is a sort of second cousin to the russified Stolz[29] with the difference that he springs from Russian soil and grows up amid the din and clatter of machines.

We have had occasion to note the social unrest of the late fifties as expressed in *Fathers and Children,* and in the sixties, as suggested by *Smoke.* This unrest took a sharper form in the seventies, when it ripened into the movement for a broader form of democracy. In *Virgin Soil* Turgenev deals with the revolutionary activities actuated by a number of young men and women who went into the Russian Villages to conduct revolutionary propaganda among the peasants. They took up the slogan "toward the people" idealizing the common man, believing at the same time that the Russian village community contained the beginnings of a better social order. They tried to adopt the same mode of living as the peasants.

The movement was crude and disorganized and rather naïve. This fact was brought out excellently in Turgenev's novel. Nevertheless the enthusiasm, the sincerity and the deep devotion to the cause was treated with broad sympathy. The psychology of the revolutionary heroes as well as that of the bureaucrats was studied with a view to depicting the opposing elements. The action is referred to the late sixties. Turgenev was now more and more overwhelmed by the all-pervading want of the Russian people. Poverty, squalor, rags, was what he saw about him. He was very pessimistic and could hardly believe that all this inarticulate endurance would ever ripen into the revolt of action.

The hero Nezhdanov, a young university student of noble but illegitimate descent, has his sympathies roused for the oppressed peasantry of Russia, and with romantic ardor enters into a secret conspiracy for their relief. It is a time when half of Russia is dying of hunger; students' benefit clubs have been closed; spies are everywhere along with oppression, lies, betrayals, deceit. He feels that he ought to do something. He knows, however, next to nothing of the Russian people for whose benefit the revolution is to be effected. He

---

[29] Goncharov, *Oblomov.*

has inherited an "aristocratic" vein from his father and so is not really "one of the people." "I see that you are not a democrat in spite of your being a revolutionist!" says the satirical Paklin.[30]

Nezhdanov is engaged as a tutor by a government official and "pillar of society," a certain Sipyagin, who in the guise of a Russian Liberal has retained all his sympathies for the government stick. At his house the young student meets Marianna, a relation of the family, who is also secretly an enthusiast in the Nihilistic cause. Her very nature breathes revolt. She is out of sympathy with everybody and everything in this well-ordered house, where she is a dependent. She, too, longs passionately to do something for Russia. Her "benefactors" wish to marry her off to another "pillar," Kalomyeytsev, who has taken a two months' leave to look after his estate, that is, to threaten and oppress his peasants a little more. His theory is that "you can't get on without that!" He is an upstart and seems to be introduced with a view of pointing out a type of champion of the old system who did not really know the old régime except on its inhuman side. Being cruel meant to him acting the lord who followed the enlightened principle of "spare the rod and spoil the peasant." He is little more than Tikhon Ilyich (Krasov) in Bunin's *Village,* except that he has adopted the outward veneer of polite society. Kalomeytsev would abolish county councils. According to him they only weakened the government and set people thinking the wrong way. He takes no interest in Russian literature because of its assuming "vulgar" aspects: "A cook is now made the heroine of a novel."[31] He does not mind Marianna's interesting herself in the woman question, only he would forbid such things being talked about; at least, through the press. He would give utterance to the most retrogressive opinions, proposing a toast "I drink to the only principle I acknowledge, the whip."[32]

Of course, Marrianne despises him. She falls in love with Nezhdanov. The latter, who is another character of Turgenev's gallery of Hamlets, instinctively feels that he will never be able to realize her

[30] R. S. Townsend's trans., p. 13. *Sochineniya.* IV, 16.

[31] *Sochineniya.* IV, 40; Townsend, p. 37.

[32] *Ibid.,* IV. 52; Townsend, p. 49.

expectations for action demanded of him. He is a dreamer, whom destiny has thrown into a stream he is ill-adapted to control. He loves Marianna and is honest enough to make a brave attempt. He will join hands with her and they will work for "the cause." She suffers for the miserable, poor, and oppressed in the whole of Russia: "I suffer—I am indignant for them, I rebel for them.—I am ready to go to the stake for them."[33]

But is he really the man who would benefit "the cause"? Did he feel that straining of the whole being, that longing to be amongst the first ranks, which is inspired by the approach of the battle? No. Did he believe in this cause? He was too much of an aesthetic and too much of a skeptic. If he is such a melancholy dreamer, what sort of revolutionist will he make? He ought to amuse himself with psychological fancies and subtleties of all sorts, but not mistake his sickly, nervous irritability for the manly wrath of conviction. "O Hamlet! Hamlet! thou Prince of Denmark! How escape from the shadow of thy spirit?" In this apostrophe we hear again Turgenev's voice, which we have heard so often before, waking Russian Youth into action.

But do others know what they are about? Very few of them do. Will the salvation come from men like Kislyakov who, in his twelve-page letters, always speaks of his unsparing activity, who

in one month had been in no less than eleven provinces, in nine towns, in twenty-nine villages, fifty-three hamlets, in one farm-house, and in seven factories; who had written fourteen long letters, twenty-eight shorter ones, and eighteen notes, four of which were written in pencil, one in blood, and another in soot and water.[34]

Or, is one to expect much from the vulgar rants of Golushkin or even Markelov, who means immediate action. We get a suggestion of what was going on at a meeting of the members of "the cause."

Like the first flakes of snow whirling round and round in the mild autumn air, so words began flying in all direction; all kinds of words, rolling and tumbling over one another: progress, government, literature, the taxation

---

[33] Townsend. p. 97; *Sochineniya*. IV, 103.
[34] *Ibid.*, p. 118; *Sochineniya*. IV, 125.

question, realism, nihilism, communism, international, clerical, liberal, capital, administration, organization, association, and even crystallization![35]

To some this uproar seemed the real thing. And yet though their analysis may be mere verbiage, what counts is—faith in the cause. Kislyakov's letters may be nonsense, but, says Markelov "he *believes* in our cause, believes in the revolution! And I must say that you are very luke-warm . . . you *don't believe* in our cause!"[36] Markelov argues for action without delay.

If we have to wait until everything, absolutely everything is ready, we shall never make a beginning. If we weigh all the consequences beforehand we are sure to find some bad ones among them. For instance, when our forefathers emancipated the serf, do you think they could foresee that a whole class of money-lending landlords would spring up as a result of the emancipation? You'll agree that our emancipators could hardly have foreseen that. Even if they had foreseen it, they would still have been quite right in freeing the serfs without weighing all the consequences beforehand![37]

Were it not far Marianna, Nezhdanov would continue hamletising. Her words give him courage and momentary faith. "We shall succeed, you will see, we'll be useful, our life won't be wasted. We'll go among the people."[38] She is preparing to run away with Nezhdanov. "The great work is about to begin—and am I to remain in this house, where everything is deceit and falsehood? People I love will be exposed to danger and I—"[39] On the eve of elopement Nezhdanov writes to his friend Silin:

I need not tell you what we are going for and what we have chosen to do. Marianna and I are not in search of happiness or vain delight; we want to enter the fight together, side by side, supporting each other. Our aim is clear to us, but we do not know the roads that lead to it. Shall we find, if not help and sympathy, at any rate the opportunity to work?[40]

They elope. Solomin, their friend, offers them a room in the factory of which he is a manager. They wish to come into closer touch

[35] *Ibid.*, p. 152; *Sochineniya*, IV, 159.   [36] *Ibid.*, p. 156; *Sochineniya*. IV, 163.
[37] *Ibid.*, p. 160; *Sochineniya*. IV, 168.   [38] *Ibid.*, p. 171; *Sochineniya*. IV, 180
[39] *Ibid.*, p. 195; *Sochineniya*. IV, 295.   [40] *Ibid.*, p. 208; *Sochineniya*. IV, 220.

with "the people." Marianna wants to rid herself of her "lady-like" manners. She wants to become "simplified." They have not learned yet what that implies. Tatyana, Solomin's housekeeper, looks at them with sympathy saying: "You are taking a heavier burden on your shoulders than you can bear. It's people like you that the Tsar's folk are ready to put into prison."[41]

Nezhdanov disguised as a peddler goes to distribute leaflets among the peasants. The first day turns out disappointing. He wonders whether his efforts were worth while. He discovers that absolutely everyone he comes across is discontented, but no one cares to find out the remedy for this discontent. Of the men to whom he offered the pamphlets, one asked whether it was a religious book and refused to take it; the second could not read, but took it home to his children for the sake of the picture on the cover; the third abused him soundly; the fourth did take one, but he proved to be a half-crazed individual.

To become "simplified" he had to join in with others and drink vodka, which he detested. "It is difficult for aesthetic creatures like me to come in contact with real life,"[42] he concludes. In the evening he writes to his friend Silin:

I have been going "among the people," and really it would be impossible to imagine anything more stupid than they are. I want to influence them. But how? How can it be done? I feel that I am a bad actor in a part that does not suit him. Conscientiousness or skepticism are absolutely of no use.[43]

He realizes the futility of his efforts and is disgusted with his rôle.

It is worse than useless! I find it disgusting to look at the filthy rags I carry about on me. They say you must first learn the language of the people, their habits and customs, but rubbish, rubbish, rubbish, I say! You have only to *believe* in what you say and say what you like![44]

There is something tragic in this attitude of Nezhdanov's, typical of many of Turgenev's *lishnie lyudi* ("superfluous people"). He saw

[41] *Ibid.*, p. 224; *Sochineniya.* IV, 236.
[42] *Ibid.*, p. 241; *Sochineniya.* IV, 254.
[43] *Ibid.*, p. 239; *Sochineniya.* IV, 252.
[44] *Ibid.*, p. 239; *Sochineniya.* IV, 252.

no outlet, no purpose in life, but one—to serve the people by going among them. In this object he failed. But this giving-up attitude was hardly justifiable in Nezhdanov's case. He was on the threshold of the 80's, when there began to be a growing recognition of "Art for Art's Sake" and a field for action of Nezhdanov's aesthetic stamp was not impossible. He confined himself, however, to activities he was little fit for; hence the maladjustment that resulted. In going among the people, as he understood his mission, he had little use for the refinements of sense that his aristocratic birth gave him.

How I loathe this irritability, sensitiveness, impressionableness, fastidiousness, inherited from my aristocratic father! What right had he to bring me into this world, endowed with qualities quite unsuited to the sphere in which I must live? An aesthetic amidst filth! A democrat, a lover of the people, yet the very smell of their filthy vodka makes me feel sick![45]

If any one does listen to him readily and does take his pamphlets at once, he is sure to be of an undesirable brainless sort. Moreover, he notices now the appearance of "superfluous people" among the peasants. These village Hamlets are ineffective, as far as the "cause" is concerned.

In all this we can almost hear Turgenev's voice crying bitter disappointment. Characteristic is the following hint at the repressions of the press: "What can one do? Should one write novels of peasant life with plenty of padding? They wouldn't be published, you know."[46]

That same voice coming from Turgenev's suffering heart at the slow march of progress in Russia we hear in Nezhdanov's concluding poem "Sleep."

> After a long absence I return to my native land,
> Finding no striking change there.
> The same dead, senseless stagnation;
> > crumbling houses,
> > crumbling walls,
> And the same filth, dirt, poverty, and misery.
> Unchanged the servile glance, now insolent, now dejected.

---

[45] *Ibid.*, IV, 253; Townsend, p. 240.   [46] *Ibid.*, p. 242; *Sochineniya.* IV, 255.

Free have our people become, and
    the free arm
Hangs as before like a whip unused. . . .
Holy Russia, our fatherland, lies in
    eternal sleep.[47]

"All are asleep!" runs like a refrain through the poem, only "the tavern never closes a relentless eye." "Our people are asleep,"[48] Nezhdanov writes in his *postscriptum*, summarizing the poem once more. "Will they ever awake?" is the implied question.

In spite of the low spirits he is in, Nezhdanov has the courage to try once more to go "among the people." With a grim determination to conquer his constitutional weaknesses he shouts revolutionary sentiments along the country road. The peasants stare at him in bewilderment as he shouts: "Why are you asleep? Rouse yourself! The time has come! Down with the taxes! Down with the landlords!" He got himself up into such a state of excitement that he was no longer able to distinguish sense from nonsense. He saw suddenly a group of peasants standing by the side of the road. He jumped out of the lumber cart he was on, rushed up, and began shouting; throwing out his fists and gesticulating all the time. One could now and then distinguish "For Freedom! March on! Put your shoulder to the wheel!"

In the next village a gigantic muzhik dragged him into a tavern. There he is made to drink their horrible vodka. Nezhdanov drinks glass after glass with a desperate heroism till the vodka fairly maddens him. The earth seems reeling under his feet. The peasants eventually lose patience with him, handle him roughly, shout at him as he staggers into the cart to be driven back whence he came.

When consciousness eventually comes back to him the idealized vision he entertained before loses all its glamour. He can no longer attempt to deceive himself. Reality comes back with all its unvarnished aspect. On one side there is a mere handful of thinkers, all more or less incapable of any sustained, concentrated action, but faithful to their ideals, eager for sacrifice, however useless and how-

[47] *Ibid.*, p. 243; *Sochineniya.* IV, 257.
[48] *Ibid.*, p. 244; *Sochineniya.* IV, 258.

ever sordid. Opposed to these are millions of perfectly contented people who shake them off. Markelov is arrested by the very people he is trying to better. They tie his hands, fling him into a cart, and bring him to the governor. Ostrodumov is killed by a shopkeeper he is inciting to revolt. The Russian peasant who was kept under heel for so many centuries could never be induced to revolt except by one's taking advantage of his devotion to some high authority, to some Tsar. Some sort of legend must be invented, some sort of royal sign must be shown to him. Hence, this isolated group of dreamers carry no message to the bulk of the people.

Nezhdanov realizes only too well that his effort to descend to the level of the peasants, to enter into their life and to rouse them to a united movement for liberty, has been met with a stolid apathy and lack of intelligence on their part. This is enough to dampen his ardor and to make his efforts seem to him like the merest sentimentalism, that can never yield any real result. This loss of faith in himself and in his own sincerity impels him to break his promise of marriage with Marianna, and, asking her to marry Solomin he puts a bullet through his head, in despair of finding a sphere in the world for his genius—a mixture of inherited aristocracy and purely romantic democracy. An "idealist of realism" he was, says Mashurina.

As in other novels, so in *Virgin Soil* the Hamlet of the story has his antithesis. In this case it is Solomin, the factory manager. For a number of years he lived in England and caught the practical spirit of the English race. What Russia needs, according to him, is not great heroes of the Robespierre type, but a patient laborious people who would teach the alphabet to children and orderliness in the home to parents. He outlines to Marianna the mission of Woman:

Today you will begin teaching some Lukeria something good for her, and a difficult matter it will be, because you won't understand your Lukeria and she won't understand you, and on top of it she will imagine that what you are teaching is of no earthly use to her. In two or three weeks you will try your hands on another Lukeria, and meanwhile you will be washing a baby here, teaching another the alphabet, or handing some sick man his medicine.—And there is a chance for self-sacrifice . . . combing the scurfy heads of gutter children is a sacrifice; a great sacrifice of which not many people are capable. You will be washing pots and plucking chickens. . . . And who knows, maybe you will save your country in that way![49]

In this work of saving the country, woman stands much higher than man, he thinks. "You Russian women are more capable and higher than we men."[50]

Solomin's aims are the same as Markelov's, Nezhdanov's and the other revolutionists', but his method is different. For Russia it is beneficial to have factory managers like himself, so he is doing his duty as a patriot by avoiding Siberia and keeping his head on his shoulders. He is nevertheless moving steadily onwards. Later on he establishes a factory on coöperative lines. "Solomin's strength lies in the fact that he doesn't attempt to cure all the social ills with one blow," says Paklin.[51] The Solomins do not make heroes, but they are robust, strong people and are what a country needs. A head as clear as the day and a body as strong as an ox. "Our true salvation lies with the Solomins, the dull, plain, but wise Solomins! Remember that I say this to you in the winter of 1870.—"[52] are Paklin's concluding remarks.

Turgenev believed in the final deliverance of the Russian soul. He expressed the faith that was in him, not through the lips of men but through the lips of Russian women. They are the quiet, steadfast women, asking nothing for themselves, seeking only to give. For them Turgenev has a reverence beyond words of praise. In no one of his books has a woman hesitated on the eve of action. Everything that Turgenev denied to his weak men he granted abundantly to his heroines, whose love was inseparable from sacrifice. Such is Marianna in *Virgin Soil*.

The "Fomushka and Fimushka" episode[53] has apparently for its purpose to throw into relief the fitful actions of the revolutionists. Though we are in the seventies of the nineteenth century, Fomushka and Fimushka still live in the eighteenth century. On their modest estate things are at a standstill. "That is what we are likely to become

---

[49] Townsend, p. 233; *Sochineniya*. IV, 246.
[50] *Ibid.*, p. 233; *Sochineniya*. IV, 247. [51] *Ibid.*, p. 318; *Sochineniya*. IV, 334.
[52] *Ibid.*, p. 319; *Sochineniya*. IV, 335. [53] *Sochineniya*. IV, 137-53.

if we remain inactive," is the silent message we read in the childlike characters of Fomushka and Fimushka. They represent the real old type Russian family who kept up the good and the bad sides of a bygone epoch. And yet they are the only ones who are honest with themselves. They act out sincerely what the others are only talking about.

"Are they conscious of the fact that they play the part of clowns?" wondered Nezhdanov.[54] We cannot help feeling, however, that they are true philosophers, without knowing it. Theirs is a natural religion of the soul. They are serf-owners but no serf of theirs would ever wish to be included in the Emancipation Act. After all, "they are in the right," thought Nezhdanov.[55]

PUNIN AND BABURIN

Punin and Baburin, a work that Turgenev wrote about two years previous to *Virgin Soil* deserves discussion, for the author's sympathy with the fighter for freedom is clearly displayed there. In *Punin and Baburin,* we have in addition a number of autobiographical touches that are not without interest to a student of Turgenev. The author is careful to indicate the year to which the actions at different points of the story refer. The story goes back to 1830 when Turgenev was about twelve years old. According to the story, he lived then with his irascible grandmother.

But in the portrait he drew of her we have little difficulty in recognizing his mother before whom the footman would appear, his lips tightly compressed, "in order that he might not infect the air with his breath."[56] Into this household comes Baburin as a scribe in the office. We are given to understand at the very start that Baburin, though of plebeian stock, has "advanced" notions. He does not like to be addressed in terms of "thou." In his attitude he implies that economic inequality does not lower the dignity of the poor. Baburin knows his worth as a human being. He is bold enough to tell the despotic landlady that he does not permit corporal punishment upon peasants, although this assertion may mean his losing his chance of

---

[54] *Ibid.,* IV, 149.   [55] *Ibid.,* IV, 149.
[56] *Ibid.,* VIII, 37; Hapgood. X, 282.

securing a position which would mean economic security for him and for his friend Punin, who is a sort of helpless creature.

According to Baburin, helping the poor is a "duty" for the poor but an "occupation" for the wealthy.[57]

Throughout the book we are summoned to witness that the poor may have loftier souls than the rich. It is Baburin again who stands up for their rights. When the young master enters his room freely, he is told that though he is the proprietress's grandson, he must be taught a lesson: "I know my duties, and I also know my rights very well."[58] Baburin was the type who knew how to live up to his convictions.

For a man like Baburin to retain a position in a house where extreme despotism was a religion would be a marvel. The clash between him and the proprietress came only too soon. It was caused by an incident with a serf, referred to earlier.[59] In passing a group of house-serfs the proprietress noticed one of them doffing his cap reluctantly. Perhaps he was thinking of the injustice done to his father! For some ten years previous to that his father, who was majordomo in the house and enjoyed the mistress' special favor, had suddenly fallen into disfavor, had been converted into a herdsman and then, descending still further, had became a tender of fowl on an allowance of thirty-six pounds of flour a month. He had died of paralysis.

It is this hapless man's son that the proprietress now spied. "We shall have to take measures about that fellow. I don't want any people around who gaze askance at me." Three hours later the young fellow was being sent off to Siberia for colonization.

Beyond the fence, a few paces distant from him, a wretched little peasant-cart, laden with his poor effects, was visible. That was the way things went in those days!—Emil stood capless, with drooping head, bare-footed, his boots bound with a rope slung behind his back; his face turned toward the mistress' manor-house, expressed neither despair nor grief, nor even surprise; a stupid grin had congealed on his colorless lips.[60]

They had been trained into suffering and dared not even complain! But there was a man who did dare—Baburin. It might mean months

[57] *Ibid.*, VIII, 40; Hapgood. X, 285. [58] *Ibid.*, VIII, 47; Hapgood. X, 296.
[59] See Ch. II, p. 13.
[60] Hapgood. X, 307; *Sochineniya*. VIII, 54.

of misery to him and his friend, but he had to have his say, when justice was involved and when the cause of the oppressed was to be championed! "Such measures," he rang out in hoarse, choking voice "lead only to dissatisfaction and to other consequences,—and are nothing else than excesses of the power conferred upon landed proprietors."[61] The answer Baburin gets is worthy of the lady whose will is law:

So my arrangements do not please thee. That is not of the slightest consequences to me; I can dispose of my subjects as I see fit, and I am not answerable to any one of them; only I am not accustomed to have people argue in my presence, and meddle with what does not concern them; I need no philanthropic plebeians. I lived thus before I knew thee, and I shall continue thus to live after thy time also. I have no further use for thee; thou art discharged.[62]

Upon leaving, Baburin has a parting word of advice for the young master. "Here is a lesson for you, young sir; remember today's doings, and when you grow up try to put an end to such injustice."[63] Punin is not behind his friend and declaims to the boy Derzhavin's paraphrase of a psalm of David:

> How long, saith He, how long shall ye
> Be spared, ye evil and unjust!
> It is your duty to uphold the laws,
> Your duty to preserve th' innocent from want,
> To furnish shelter to th' unfortunate,
> And from the powerful to protect the weak.[64]

People of Baburin's type are much ahead of their time and are bound to meet with reverses at every corner. He is branded as a "republican." Although the term is used in the story in a somewhat disparaging sense, Baburin's actions lend to it the noblest significance. To him a republic is an organization founded on law and justice; an institution where no one can force another person and

---

[61] *Ibid.*, V, 307; *Sochineniya.* VIII, 55.
[62] *Ibid.*, X, 306; *Sochineniya.* VIII, 56.
[63] *Ibid.*, X, 310; *Sochineniya.* VIII, 57.
[64] *Ibid.*, X, 311; *Sochineniya.* VIII, 58.

where everyone can dispose of himself freely.[65] This is what he said to Muza, his ward, whom he wished to marry, but who had her affections settled elsewhere. She learned her lesson in life, however, and years later came back to Baburin to share his unenviable lot, to roam with him from post to post and to accept the good or bad that the coming day had in reserve for them.

For a short time fortune smiled upon them. Baburin obtained a post in private service, in Petersburg. Before long he ran into an unpleasantness with his employer because he took it into his head to stand up for the workmen. He remained faithful to his convictions under the most trying obstacles. The despotic order could only strengthen these convictions and spur him on to action much sooner. That was one year after the disturbances of 1848. Failures of democratic attempts could not break the spirit of Baburin. Like the giant Antaeus he felt stronger after each downfall. If the present offered no consolation, the future was still before him. "What are they doing now with the young people?—Why, assuredly, in the end that will break down all patience. . . . Break it! Yes, just wait a bit!"[66]

Shortly after this Baburin was arrested and imprisoned. All books and letters were sealed. Muza felt it her mission to stand by his side and alleviate his lot. He was exiled to Siberia for colonization. We hear of him again twelve years later, in 1861, one month after the Peasant Emancipation. He and his wife Muza had been busying themselves with the organization of schools. Upon hearing of the manifesto he exclaims: "This is the first step; it must be followed by others."[67] A few months after that Baburin died. Muza remained in Siberia, continuing her mission of enlightening the unlettered folk.

When Turgenev wrote this work he was approaching his sixties. He could never rid himself of pressing reminiscences of events that were part and parcel of his life and his happiness. And so, in a series of shifting scenes he once more brought before us the picture of old days, the heartlessness of those in power and the effect upon the fighting spirit of those who had the courage to protest.

[65] *Ibid.*, X, 361; *Sochineniya.* VIII, 85.
[66] *Ibid.*, X, 371; *Sochineniya.* VIII, 99.
[67] *Ibid.*, X, 380; *Sochineniya.* VIII, 105.

Turgenev's sympathy with the peasants remained through life. The injustices perpetrated against them left so deep a scar upon his sensitive soul that even after the Emancipation Laws he would revert to them. In "Zhivya moshchi" ("Living Relics") (1872), which became incorporated in the *Sketches* in a later edition, he shows the depth of sentiment and great power of resignation the serfs are capable of. The Christ-like readiness to forgive, the readiness to see good in the world, after all, raises the poor invalid almost to sublimity.

References to the serf-laws are found in *Spring Freshets* (1871). Sanin is speaking to Frau Leonore about his prospects. He purposes selling his estate "Does that mean that you will sell the peasants also?" she asks. The poor young man feels as though he had been stabbed in the ribs, for on a previous occasion he asserted that he regarded such sale as an immoral act. Shortly after that we find him negotiating with Countess Pólozoff about the price per peasant at five hundred rubles per soul. On other occasions we find hints in the conversations of characters. So Countess Pólozoff in speaking about her freedom-loving nature ends with the remarks: "I must have seen a great deal of slavery in my childhood, and have suffered much from it."[68]

Sometimes we see malice in the hints suggesting Russian despotism: "—Good people get sent to Siberia, better men than you and I...." says the indignant David to his uncle, when accused of stealing.[69]

A discussion about Turgenev's democratic ideas would hardly be complete without saying a few words concerning his *Poems in Prose* that were written within five years of his death and that represent the conclusions of a mature mind. The philosophic reflections they suggest, the boundless sympathy they inspire, along with the remarkably simple and poetic style in which they are couched, make each of them a sparkling gem.

The gospel of brotherhood of all mankind is suggested in most of these. There are no high-born and low-born, is the lesson to be

---

[68] *Ibid.*, XV, 205; *Sochineniya.* VIII, 435.
[69] *Ibid.*, XV, 357; *Sochineniya* VIII, 151.

learned from "The Beggar."[70] When the decrepit old beggar, in coarse rags, holds out his swollen filthy hand, with its festering wounds, the author discovers he has nothing to offer him. Confused and abashed he warmly clasps the filthy hand: "Don't be angry, brother; I have nothing, brother." The beggar in turn grips his fingers: "What of it, brother? Thanks for this, too. That is a gift, too, brother." The author feels that he, too, had received a gift from his brother. What a breadth of sympathy in so few words! No lengthy essays on morals could tell more than is conveyed by Turgenev's terse suggestion.

His philosophy of Universal Love embraces both man and beast. Before Mother Nature both are of the same rank. "There are two of us in the room, my dog and I. We look into each other's eyes, he says, speaking of the dog.[71] "There is living in him the same feeling. We are the same; in each of us there burns and shines the same trembling spark."[72]

A similar beginning do we find in "On the Sea."[73] "There were two passengers on the boat, myself and a little monkey." The wretched little monkey who during a sea storm clings to him, provokes a feeling of warmth: "We are all children of one mother, and I was glad that the poor little beast was soothed and that it nestled so confidingly up to me, as to a brother."[74]

Love for the weak is made frequently the theme in these *Prose Poems*. It is dealt with most artistically in "The Sparrow."[75] A hunter watched his dog's tracking a game. The animal noticed a young sparrow, which had fallen out of the nest, and which was unable to move. An old sparrow in a tree close by, saw the slow approach of the dog, when it suddenly darted, flinging itself toward the open jaws of the dog. It sprang to save the little sparrow. Its tiny body was shaking with terror. "What a huge monster must the dog have seemed to it!" exclaims Turgenev. "And yet it could not

---

[70] *Sochineniya*. VIII, 360; Garnett. X, 250.
[71] Garnett, X, 247; *Sochineniya*, VIII, 358.
[72] *Ibid.*, X, 247; *Sochineniya*. VIII, 358.
[73] *Sochineniya*. VIII, 406; Garnett X, 319.
[74] *Loc. cit.*   [75] *Ibid.*, VIII, 374; X, 269.

keep out of danger and remain in safety on the branch. A force stronger than its will flung it down." Even the dog was made to take a step back. He recognized this powerful force, as it were. "Love," adds the author "is stronger than death, or the fear of death. *Only by love,* life holds together and advances."

Sometimes Turgenev launches into the general field of morals. That the good man is not necessarily he who is faultless, we are told in "The Egoist":

Complacent in the sense of his own conscientiousness, he crushed every one with it,—his family, his friends and his acquaintances. . . . Not recognizing the smallest weakness in himself he did not tolerate any weakness in any one. . . . He did not even understand the meaning of forgiveness. He had never had to forgive himself.

That sort of virtue is despotic! It is almost worse than vice! "Oh, hideousness of self-complacent, unbending, cheaply bought virtue; thou art almost more revolting than the frank hideousness of vice!"[76] Nor is the religious enthusiast a model for humanity, one concludes from "The Monk." "Let him understand me and not condemn me. . . . He has found wherein to forget himself . . . but I, too, find the same. He does not lie . . . but neither do I lie."[77]

That good is of the highest sort which is done for its own sake, in spite of unfavorable judgment coming from the crowd. This is suggested by "Thou Shalt Hear the Fool's Judgment."

There are blows which pierce cruelly to the very heart. . . . A man has done all that he could; has worked strenuously, lovingly, honestly. . . . And honest hearts turn from him in disgust. . . . "We have no need of you, nor of your work. You know us not and understand us not. . . . You are our enemy!" What is that man to do? Go on working; not try to justify himself, and not even look forward to a fairer judgment.

At one time the tillers of the soil cursed the traveller who brought the potato, the substitute for bread, the poor man's daily food. Now they are fed with it.[78]

The merit in doing good is in proportion to the amount of personal sacrifice. "Rothschild is a long way behind the peasant!" exclaims

[76] Garnett. X, 294-95; *Sochineniya.* VIII, 391.

[77] *Ibid.,* X, 321; VIII, 409.   [78] *Ibid.,* X, 251; *Sochineniya.* VIII, 361.

Turgenev, commenting upon the poverty-stricken peasant who took a poor orphan into his tumble-down hut. "There won't now be enough to get us salt for our bread," remarked his wife. "Well . . . we'll do without salt," answered the peasant.[79]

In a symbolic way we are reminded that Love and Hunger are twin brothers: "Love and Hunger—twin brothers, the two foundation-stones of all things living. All that lives moves to get food, and feeds to bring forth young. Love and Hunger—their aim is one; that life should not cease, the life of the individual and the life of others."[80]

As a rule, those who do good for the sake of reward find disappointment. When Lady Benevolence was introduced to Lady Gratitude at the Banquet of the Supreme Being, the two Virtues looked at each other in amazement; for, ever since the world had stood, this was the first time they had met.[81]

The conflict between despotism and the oppressed has not been overlooked in the *Prose Poems*. "Necessitas-Vis-Libertas"[82] symbolizes the populace driven by the oppressors. The tall bony woman with an iron face and dull fixed look may be interpreted as the Russian State holding the people in its iron grasp. Its determinations are fixed and untouched by sympathy. This woman is pushing another woman before her, which may represent Bureaucracy acting in an executive capacity. The second woman is of huge stature, powerful, thickset, having the muscles of a Hercules, with a tiny head set on a bull neck, and blind. This woman in turn pushes before her a small thin girl. The meaning is quite apparent. The large force comprising the executive machinery of the Russian government is a Hercules in power, but has very little brains of its own. It is blind. It knows not what it does. It merely supplies muscular driving power. What can the poor little girl, representing the people do, driven as she is by the two grim monsters behind her? She alone has eyes that see; she wants to resist but finds herself unable. She must yield and go where she is driven.

---

[79] "Two Rich Men." Garnett. X, 288; *Sochineniya*. VIII, 388.
[80] "The Two Brothers." Garnett, X, 291; *Sochineniya*. VIII, 389.
[81] *Sochineniya* VIII, 393; Garnett, X, 296.
[82] *Ibid.*, VIII, 382; X, 280.

The heartlessness of military authorities is eloquently featured in the little story "Hang Him," referred to the year 1803.[83] A woman complains to a passing general that one of the soldiers stole a hen. Without much ado the general makes a rapid end of the matter. "Hang him!" he bawls out and rides off. The poor fellow is seized and led off to execution. The woman did not expect this termination and is extremely horrified. But discipline must be upheld!

In "We Will Still Fight On"[84] despotism is represented as a hawk hovering over a family of sparrows ready, perhaps, at any moment to swoop down and devour one from their midst. A brave little fellow was chirping saucily, as if he were not afraid of any one! But just the same "we will fight on, and damn it all!"

In three of his *Poems* he pays tribute to the fighter for freedom. These fighters must be ready to run dangers for an ungrateful crowd. Very few of them see the fruits of their labor. This lack of appreciation is shown in "The Workman and the Man with the White Hands."[85] Says the fighter: ". . . Because I worked for your good, tried to set free the oppressed and the ignorant, stirred folks up against your oppressor, resisted the authorities, they locked me up." *The Workman:* "Locked you up, did they? Serves you right for resisting." Two years pass. The same "Man with the White Hands" is to be hung for resisting the authorities. All that the workmen are interested in is the getting of a bit of rope they are going to hang him with. "They say, it brings good luck to a house!"

In "To the Memory of U. P. Vrevskaya,"[86] Turgenev speaks of the girl who gave herself up to the cause of the people: A soft, tender heart . . . and such force, such eagerness for sacrifice. To help those who needed help . . . she knew of no other happiness. All aglow with the fire of unquenchable faith, she gave herself to the service of her neighbors. And yet there is hardly anyone to appreciate these sacrifices. "Grievous it is to think that no one said thanks even to her dead body, though she herself was shy and shrank from all thanks." "On the Threshold"[87] expresses in most poetical terms his

[83] *Ibid.,* VIII, 402; Garnett X, 310.   [84] *Ibid.,* VIII, 410; X, 323.

[85] Garnett. X, 271; *Sochineniya.* VIII, 375.   [86] *Ibid.,* X, 275; VIII, 379.

[87] This poem first appeared in *Narodnaya Volya* ("The Popular Will"), in 1883.

admiration for those women who gave their lives for the revolutionary movement and went on the scaffold, without being even understood at the time by those for whom they died.

> Do you know what awaits you?
> I do.
> Cold, hunger, hatred, derision, prison, sickness, even death?
> I know.
> Estrangement, complete loneliness?
> I know. I am ready to endure all sufferings.
> Are you ready to sacrifice, to sacrifice anonymously, to perish, without even being remembered?
> I need neither thanks nor regrets.

This poem was devoted to the girl-revolutionist Sofia Perovska, who was shot down by the government.

Although in his correspondence Turgenev took a sharp stand against revolutionary methods and aims, he, nevertheless, always retained and idealized pictures of the fighter for freedom who is misunderstood by the people to whose welfare he sacrifices his own, and who is hunted down by the powers of organized despotism.

The *Prose Poems* are not devoid of a mystical element which appears in them in the form of an intuitive fathoming of the depth of life's meaning. No picture of Turgenev would be complete without taking into account this mystical wave which swept upon him during the last fifteen years of his life and which colored some of his writings. Already in 1863 the mystical element is suggested in the fantastic pictures of "Phantoms." It is strongly apparent in "The Dog" (1866), and grows more prominent as years go on. We see it in "A Strange Story" (1869), which traces the hypnotic influence upon a girl of an ignorant semi-idiotic man, who passes as a saint. It comes up again in "Knock . . . Knock . . . Knock" (1871), where a nervous individual is led to commit suicide in response to a call from the spirit of a girl toward whom he acted a mean part. In "The Dream" (1876), the fanciful and the real seem blended; a young man identifies his father by the resemblance he bears to the man he dreamt about. The main interest in "Father Alexey's Story" (1877), depends upon mysterious presences. Although told in the form of a fairy tale,

"The Song of Triumphant Love" (1881) shows by the occult powers that are prominent in the development of the plot, that the mystical tendencies continue to have a strong hold on the writer's mind. This tendency is most prominent in "Clara Milich" (1883), written during the last year of his life. It is the work of a practically disordered mind plagued by visions to which he is attempting to give objective reality. It was written during moments of relief from the terrible pains occasioned by the rapidly developing cancer of the spine.

CHAPTER VII

CONCLUSION

In our attempt to trace the democratic ideas in Turgenev's works it was our desire to look for the genesis of the various notions that found their way into the writer's mind. We saw that the roots lay back in the previous century and possibly earlier, in conditions that gave rise to serfdom in Russia. We saw how the entire social order was colored by the system that divided society into two sharp classes, the owners of "souls," and the serfs who were owned. It was a strange contradiction of terms to speak of these as "souls," for the spiritual demands of the serfs, their "souls" were least considered.

If writers like Pushkin or Krylov kept up their optimism under conditions that an enlightened mind would dislike, it was apparently because they found it convenient to live in a state of unquestioning acceptance of the comforts that life offered. An occasional protest like that of Novikov or Radishchev was but a voice in the desert. Not until the mid-nineteenth century was that protest beginning to take definite hold on the leading minds, the idealists of the forties. It was amid these idealists that Turgenev took his place. We saw him amid circles of the intelligentsia youth, in the society of Byelinsky, Granovsky, Stankevich, Hertsen, Bakunin. These were individuals who dared deviate from the stereotyped fashions of thinking and who had courage to voice their opinions. From them Turgenev caught the spirit of democracy and the desire to see the freedom of the oppressed serf was fanned into a flame that was never to die within him. That desire was already in him, when as a child, he saw the treatment of the serfs on his mother's estate. We saw how he vowed to fight the enemy Serfdom (Chapter II), how he preferred to stay abroad in order not to sink into the spirit of unquestioning comfort, so that he might be better in the position to fight his enemy effectively.

His first literary efforts in the early forties—his plays and poems—show cautious gropings. Only here and there do we find hints thrown out against the inhumanity of the serf-owners. These hints grow bolder in the later forties, when his first sketches of the *Diary* appear. By that time other writers begin to espouse the cause of the poor and the downtrodden. Grigorovich's *Village* and *Anton Goremyka* take up the cause of the peasant.

Turgenev's first bold stroke was his "Mumu," in which the cruelty of a landed proprietress is eloquently brought before the reader. Shortly after that his *Diary of a Sportsman* appeared. The cumulative effect of these sketches was powerful and unequalled by any previous work. This was followed in rapid succession by four of his great social novels in which Turgenev's art reached its peak. It is in these novels that the men of the forties are brought before us, their strivings analyzed, their attitude toward the people traced, and the progress of democracy shown.

The *Sketches* were of a destructive nature, pointing out the evils of the old system. He is now interested in the building up process. He brings before us a line of public leaders. Among these there are some who talk a great deal but do little. They are the Rudins, who are too much absorbed in their idealism. But they are necessary, nevertheless: for, if they are not active themselves, they have in them the power to fire others to action and to advance the cause of the people.

In his *Nobleman's Nest* the hero keeps less aloof from the people and gives greater promise of action. He is a transitional type who goes a step beyond Rudin. Whereas Rudin is cosmopolitan in his attitude, Lavretsky is a Slavophile and stands for nationalization in the broadest sense. As such, he likes to see democracy come from below rather than from above. He came from abroad in order to live among the people and be one of them.

The analysis of *On the Eve,* the next great novel, brought us in contact with Insarov, a champion of the people's cause. He is the man of few words, one who goes directly toward his goal. His goal is to free his oppressed people: outside of that life has no meaning to him. His being a Bulgarian lends itself to a variety of interpretations. One critic points out that making him a Russian would mean offering a type no Russian soil would grow.[1] Turgenev justifies his choice by reference to an actual fact. However, it may have been simply an expedient to lead the censors off the scent, for during the fifties the censorship was most rigorous in Russia.

His next epoch-making work was *Fathers and Children* in which his creative genius reached its climax. The book was like a bomb sent into both the conservative and the radical camps. The main character, Bazarov, a champion of the materialistic age that was being ushered in in the sixties, is fearless in his attacks upon time-honored customs, one who takes a negative stand toward everything that cannot pass an empirical test. He is a "nihilist" in the sense of one who bows to no authority. What offended the radicals was Bazarov's boorishness, which many interpreted as an attempt to ridicule the free-thinking youth. The conservatives were touched to the quick by finding their most sacred notions questioned. Inasmuch as the book questioned everything, it implied the right to question matters of state, policies of government and the looking into the rights of the governed.

In our ideal expectations we always demand more than reality can furnish. So it was with Turgenev. The Peasant Reforms of 1861 did not satisfy him. He was filled with disappointment at the results. This disappointment was much enhanced by the way *Fathers and Children* was received by the reading public. His feelings were given expression to in a few minor works[2] and in his next novel *Smoke*. There he voices his disillusionment in his political dreams. Everything appears as smoke. With the Peasant Reforms he expected an era of many other reforms. But these were slow in coming. Many were even questioning whether the freeing of the peasant was for the better. It seems that Turgenev himself doubted that anybody at all in Russia was doing anything worth while. He accordingly, lashed all classes, especially the so called "doers" of public good.

After *Smoke* Turgenev withdrew from the field of the novel for almost a decade. However, his pen continued active in the novelette form[3] and short stories, in some of which the mystical and super-

---

[1] *Dobrolyubov.*   [2] "Phantoms; Enough."   [3] *Veshniya vody.*

natural elements begin to appear.[4] His democratic strivings are eloquently represented in *Punin and Baburin* (1874), which almost approaches socialistic propaganda. In 1876 he wrote his last great novel,
Virgin Soil, which has as its background the populist movement that
was prominent in the seventies. The noble-minded intellectual youth
conceived it their highest duty to go "among the people," to assume
a humble garb, to mingle with them, and to teach them. Nezhdanov's
experiences leave in the reader's mind a strong doubt in both the
efficacy of this method of approaching the masses as well as the fit-
ness of those who undertook the task of reforming them. In the same
work Turgenev satirized strongly the new bureaucracy and the upstart nobleman.

In all of Turgenev's novels we have noted that the women characters played a more noble part than the men. We can never forget
such types as Natalya,[5] Liza,[6] Elena,[7] Muza,[8] Marianna.[9] They are
all ready to sacrifice unhesitatingly home and the goods of life for
higher ideals. His artistic treatment, the development of the psychologic subtleties of these characters, has gained for Turgenev thousands of admirers. In Russia they became torch bearers to many a
girl who was fired with the ambition of following in their footsteps.

The last years of Turgenev's life showed him still imbued with
the spirit of freedom and the desire to see the millions happy. His
views we have shown in the analysis of his *Prose Poems*, each of
which is a nugget of wisdom containing his philosophy of life.

In our final estimate of the great writer's democratic views which
he held to the very last, it is not perhaps out of place to know what
"the people" and those coming from their ranks felt toward him.
That is shown best by a proclamation that was distributed to the
thousands attending the funeral procession in St. Petersburg, when
the body of the beloved writer was being taken to its eternal rest.
It was circulated in spite of the vigilance of the government that
made all preparations to guard against "trouble" by having a heavy

[4] "Sobaka," "Stuk . . . stuk . . . stuk," "Zhivya moshchi."
[5] *Rudin.*   [6] *Dvoryanskoe Gnyezdo.*   [7] *Nakanunye.*
[8] *Punin i Baburin.*   [9] *Nov'.*

police force along. The proclamation was written by one of the young Narodovoltsi (Free-Nationalists), P. T. Yakubovich.[10] It reads:

We can say boldly who Turgenev was and what he was for our cause. A land-proprietor by birth, an aristocrat by education and inclinations, a "gradualist" in his convictions, Turgenev, perhaps unconsciously, was in sympathy with the Russian revolution and with his tender and responsive heart he loved its promoters. Turgenev was the ideal of young generations one after another and such he will continue to be for a long while. He was the singer of unexampled and pure Russian idealism, the painter of the sufferings of the people and their inner conflicts of their soul-rending doubts, and finally of their readiness to sacrifice. The portraits of Rudin, Insarov, Elena, Bazarov, Nezhdanov, and Markelov are not only living and taken from life but types who were being imitated by our youth, types that life itself created. There were no fighters as yet for the freedom of the Russian people at the time Turgenev sketched his Insarov. Following in the steps of Bazarov an entire generation of so-called nihilists was growing up, who in their own day were an indispensable link in the development of the Russian Revolution. Without exaggeration, one may say that Turgenev's heroes have a historical significance. The deep heartache that pervades "Virgin Soil," though masked here and there by subtle irony, does not diminish our love for Turgenev. It is not the irony of the conservative camp but that of a loving heart suffering for the young generation. We do not insist on maintaining that Turgenev believed in the Russian Revolution. No, he doubted its nearness, its realization by means of heroic skirmishes with the government. Perhaps he did not even desire it and was a true "gradualist"—that is immaterial to us. What is important to us is the fact that he served the causes of the Russian Revolution by the heartfelt sentiment shown through his works. He bore a great love for the revolutionary youth and he considered them saintly victims for a holy cause. That the government holds our views regarding Turgenev's sympathies with fighters for democracy can be seen from the following official circular sent to all St. Petersburg newspapers concerning precautions in connection with the funeral:

"No publicity is to be given about the police arrangements relative to the burial of I. S. Turgenev, limiting announcements by making public only those particulars which will be published in official editions."

[10] It was reprinted in *Russkoye Bogatsvo*, (1911. Vol. IX.).

Young people carried wreaths from 176 deputations. Only three speeches were permitted at the grave, the administration being in haste to disperse the crowds as rapidly as possible. These speeches had to be submitted in due order to the censorship to forestall any "dangerous" suggestions. When the Society of Lovers of Russian Literature wished to honor the memory of Turgenev, Leo Tolstoy volunteered with an article of reminiscences, but Feoktistov, the head censor, forbade that.

Turgenev's life work was not without its beneficent influences. It roused to thought and action not only his compatriots but all Europe. He brought Russia within the compass of sympathies of other nations, gaining adherents whose number has been increasing continually, down to this very day.

CHRONOLOGICAL LIST OF TURGENEV'S WORKS

1842. THE ADVENTURES OF SUB-LIEUTENANT BUBNOV.
1843. PARASHA (Poem).
      CARELESSNESS (Play).
1844. THE CONVERSATION (Poem).
      ANDREY KOLOSOV.
      BROKE (Play).
1846. THREE PORTRAITS.
      THE BULLY.
1847. PETUSHKOV.
      WHERE IT IS THIN, THERE IT BREAKS (Play).
1848. THE FAMILY CHARGE (Play).
1849. HAMLET OF THE SHCHIGRI DISTRICT.
      THE BACHELOR (Play).
      BREAKFAST AT THE CHAIRMAN'S (Play).
1850. A MONTH IN THE COUNTRY (Play).
      DIARY OF A SUPERFLUOUS MAN.
1851. THREE MEETINGS.
1852. SPORTSMAN'S SKETCHES.
1853. TWO FRIENDS.
1854. CORRESPONDENCE.
      A QUIET BACKWATER.
1855. THE INN.
      YAKOV PASYNKOV.
      RUDIN.
1857. A TOUR IN THE FOREST.
1858. A NOBLEMAN'S NEST.
      FAUST.
1859. ON THE EVE.
      ASYA.
1860. THE FIRST LOVE.
      HAMLET AND DON QUIXOTE.

1861. FATHERS AND CHILDREN.
1863. PHANTOMS.
1864. ENOUGH.
1866. SMOKE.
       THE DOG.
1867. THE STORY OF LIEUTENANT ERGUNOV.
1868. THE UNHAPPY GIRL.
       BRIGADIER.
1869. A STRANGE STORY.
1870. KING LEAR OF THE STEPPE.
       TROPMAN'S EXECUTION.
1871. KNOCK . . . KNOCK . . . KNOCK.
       SPRING FRESHETS.
1872. LIVING RELICS.
       THE END OF CHERTOPKHANOV.
1874. PUNIN AND BABURIN.
1875. THE WATCH.
       ONE KNOCKS.
1876. VIRGIN SOIL.
       THE DREAM.
1877. FATHER ALEXEY'S STORY.
1881. OLD PORTRAITS.
       THE SONG OF TRIUMPHANT LOVE.
1882. THE DESPERATE MAN.
       POEMS IN PROSE (1878-1882).
1883. CLARA MILICH.

BIBLIOGRAPHY

RUSSIAN

ANENKOV, A. V.: *Literaturnye Vospominaniya* ("Literary Reminiscences"). St. Petersburg, 1909.

BRODSKY, M. L.: *Turgenev i ego Vremya* ("Turgenev and his Time"). Moscow, 1923.

DERMAN, A.: *Korni Turgenevskago Tvorchestva* ("The Roots of Turgenev's Creativeness"); in the periodical *Vecher*, No. 52. Kiev, 1918.

DOBROLYUBOV, N. A.: *Sochineniya*. St. Petersburg, 1901 (Edition Soykin).

DOSTOYEVSKY, FEODOR: *Byesy* ("The Possessed"). St. Petersburg, 1896.

FONVIZIN, D. I.: *Polnoye sobraniye sochinenii* (Complete Works). St. Petersburg, 1888 (Edition Shamov).

GRIBOYEDOV, A. S.: *Gore ot uma* ("Woe from Wit"). St. Petersburg, 1911.

IVANOV-RAZUMNIK: *Istoria russkoi obschestvennoi mysli* ("History of Russian Social Thought"). St. Petersburg, 1914.

—— *Russkaya literatura ot semidesyatykh godov do nashykh dney* ("Russian Literature from the Seventies to Our Days"). Berlin, 1910 (Edition Skythen).

KLYUCHEVSKY, V.: *Kurs russkoi istorii* ("A Course in Russian History"). Moscow, 1906.

KORNILOV, A.: *Kurs istorii Rossii XIX vieka* ("A Course in 19th Century History of Russia"). Moscow, 1912-14.

KOROLENKO, V.: "Turgenev i samoderzhavie" ("Turgenev and Autocracy"), in *Kievskaya mysl'*, 1918, No. 213.

KROPOTKIN, P.: *Zapiski revolutsionera* ("Notes of a Revolutionist"). Geneva, 1906.

KRYLOV, I. A.: *Polnoye sobraniye sochinenii* ("Complete Works"). St. Petersburg, 1904.

LAVROV, P.: "Turgenev i razvitie russkogo obschestva" ("Turgenev and the Development of Russian Society"). Article in *Vyestnik narodnoi voli* (The *Messenger of Popular Will*). Geneva, 1884.

L'VOV-ROGACHEVSKY, V.: "Bor'ba pokolenii" ("The Struggle of Generations"); in *Rabochi mir* (The *Worker's World*). Petrograd, 1918, Nos. 12-13.

—— *Turgenev, zhizn' i tvorchestvo* ("Turgenev, Life and Works"). Moscow, 1926.

NEZELENOV, A. I.: *Turgenev v ego proizvedeniyakh* ("Turgenev in his Works"). St. Petersburg, 1903.

OSTROVSKY, A.: *Turgenev v zapiskakh sovremennikov* ("Turgenev from Notes of his Contemporaries"). Leningrad, 1929.

—— *Polnoye sobraniye sochinenii* ("Complete Works"). St. Petersburg, 1915.

OVSYANIKOV-KULIKOVSKY: *Istoria russkoi inteligentsii* ("The History of the Russian Intelligentsia"). Moscow, 1906.

OXMAN, U. S.: *Turgenev, issledovaniya i materialy* ("Research and Source Materials"). Moscow, 1921.

PISAREV, D. I.: *Bazarov.* St. Petersburg, 1894.

—— *Pisemsky, Turgenev, Goncharov.* St. Petersburg, 1894.

—— *Realisty.* St. Petersburg, 1894.

—— *Zhenskiye tipy v romanakh i povyestyakh Pisemskago, Turgeneva i Goncharova* ("Feminine types in the novels and novellettes of Pisemsky, Turgenev, and Goncharov"). St. Petersburg, 1894.

PUSHKIN, A. S.: *Dubrovsky.* Moscow, 1899.

SAKULIN, P. N.: *Na grani dvukh kultur.* ("On the Boundary of Two Cultures"). St. Petersburg, 1902.

SEMEVSKY, V. E.: *Russki krestyanski vopros v 18 stoletii i v pervoi polovinye 19 stoletiya* ("The Peasant Question in Russia during the 18th and the First Half of the 19th Centuries"). St. Petersburg, 1888.

TALNIKOV, D.: "Turgenev i narod" ("Turgenev and the Masses"); in *Ogon'ki*, No. 26. Odessa, 1918.

TURGENEV, IVAN SERGEEVICH: *Polnoye sobraniye sochinenii* ("Complete Works"); 7th Russian Edition. Petrograd, 1915.

VENGEROV, S. A.: *Geroicheskiy kharakter russkoi literatury* ("The Heroic Character of Russian Literature"). St. Petersburg, 1911.

—— *V chem ocharovaniye russkoi literatury?* ("Wherein Lies the Charm of Russian Literature"). Petrograd, 1919.

ENGLISH

BEAZLEY, FORBES, and BIRKETT: *Russia from the Varangians to the Bolsheviks.* Oxford, 1918 (Clarendon Press).

Free Russia (periodical). Vol. XI (London).

GARNETT, EDWARD: *Turgenev, a Study.* London, 1917.

HALPERINE-KAMINSKY, E.: *Turguéneff and his French Circle*. London, 1898.

KOVALEVSKY, MAXIME: *Modern Customs and Ancient Laws of Russia*. London, 1891.

KROPOTKIN, P.: *Ideals and Realities in Russian Literature*. New York, 1909 (Alfred E. Knopf).

MANDEL, M. S.: *The Plays of Turgenev*. New York, 1924 (Macmillan).

MASARYK, THOMAS: *The Spirit of Russia*. London, 1919.

MAVOR, JAMES: *An Economic History of Russia*. New York, 1925 (Dutton & Co.).

TURGENEV: *Works*, Translation by Constance Garnet. London, 1922.

——— *Works*, Translation by Isabel F. Hapgood.

——— *Works*, Translation by I. Townsend.

WIENER, LEO: *Anthology of Russian Literature from the Earliest Period to the Present Time*. New York, 1903 (Putnam & Sons).

YARMOLINSKY, AVRAM: *Turgenev: the Man, His Art, and His Age*. New York, 1926.

FRENCH

ASHKINAZI, M. O.: *Tourguéneff inconnu*. Paris, 1888 (Librairie Illustrée).

HAUMANT, EMILE: *Ivan Tourguéneff, la vie et l'oeuvre*. Paris, 1906.

PAVLOVSKY, ISAAC: *Souvenirs sur Tourguéneff*. Paris, 1904.

STORCH, HENRI: *Cours d'économie politique, ou exposition des principes qui déterminent la prospérité des nations*. St. Petersburg, 1815.

GERMAN

STORCH, H. F.: *Historisch-statistisches Gemälde des russischen Reichs*. Leipzig, 1797-1803.

LETTERS

BATURINSKY, V. P.: *Gertsen, ego druzya i znakomye* ("Hertsen, His Friends and Acquaintances"). Contains Turgenev's letters to Hertsen. St. Petersburg, 1904.

Byloe ("The Past") (a periodical). St. Petersburg, 1906. Contains Turgenev's letters to Lavrov.

EFIMOV, I.: *Neizdannye pis'ma k gospozhe Viardo* ("Turgenev's Unpublished Letters to Mme. Viardot"), 1846-1882; 70 letters. St. Petersburg, 1900.

GEORGIEVSKY, S.: *Pis'ma Turgeneva k grafinye Lambert* ("Turgenev's Letters to Countess Lambert"), 115 letters. St. Petersburg, 1915.

GRUZINSKY I TSIAVLOVSKY: *Tolstoy i Turgenev, Perespiska* ("Correspondence between Tolstoy and Turgenev"). Moscow, 1928.

KLEMAN, M.: *Otyets Turgeneva v pis'makh k synovyam* ("Turgenev's Father in his Letters to his Sons"). In Koni's Collection, pp. 131-45. St. Petersburg, 1921.

MALYSHEV, B.: *Pis'ma Turgenevskoi materi* ("Letters of Turgenev's Mother"). In Piksanov's Collection, pp. 24-49. Moscow, 1884.

NIKOLSKY, I.: *Turgenev i Dostoyevsky, Perepiska* (Correspondence between Turgenev and Dostoyevsky"). Sofia, 1921.

Obschestvo literatorov i uchenykh ("The Society of Scholars and Literary Men"): *Sobraniye pisem Turgeneva 1840-1883* ("Collection of Turgenev's letters from 1840 to 1883") 488 letters. St. Petersburg, 1884.

POPELNITSKY, I.: In *Golos Minuvshego* ("The Voice of the Past"). Vol. 8. Contains Turgenev's letter to Alexander II. St. Petersburg, 1913.

Raduga ("The Rainbow") (a periodical): *Perepiska Turgeneva s Pisarevym* ("Correspondence between Turgenev and Pisarev"), pp. 207-25. Petrograd, 1922.

SILBERSTEIN, N.: *Dostoyevsky i Turgenev, Perepiska* ("Correspondence between Dostoyevsky and Turgenev"). Leningrad, 1928.

INDEX

COLUMBIA UNIVERSITY PRESS
COLUMBIA UNIVERSITY
NEW YORK

FOREIGN AGENT
OXFORD UNIVERSITY PRESS
HUMPHREY MILFORD
AMEN HOUSE, LONDON, E.C.